I0458676

MASTERING YOUR POTENTIAL

EMPOWERING TIPS FOR SUCCESS

RAE A. STONEHOUSE

LIVE FOR EXCELLENCE PRODUCTIONS

INTRODUCTION - UNLOCK YOUR INNER POWER

A Journey of Transformation

Imagine waking up every morning feeling energized, confident, and excited about the day ahead. Picture yourself tackling challenges with resilience, pursuing your dreams with unwavering determination, and inspiring others with your passion and positivity. This life awaits you when you unlock your inner power.

The Key to Your Potential

Within you lies an incredible force - a well of potential waiting to be tapped. It's the power to shape your thoughts, your actions, and ultimately, your reality. By harnessing this power, you can break free from limiting beliefs, overcome obstacles, and create a life that fulfills and inspires you.'

Navigating the Path

But how do you access this inner strength? How do you transform your potential into tangible results? The journey of personal growth is not always easy, but with the right tools and strategies, you can navigate the path with clarity and confidence.

Throughout this book, we'll explore the essential elements of personal mastery:

• Cultivating assertiveness and confidence to communicate clearly and pursue your goals boldly

• Enhancing your productivity through smarter habits and more focused effort

• Building rich, supportive relationships that empower your growth

• Developing resilient positivity that turns challenges into opportunities

• Aligning your life with a deeper sense of purpose that fuels your motivation

Your Roadmap to Success

Whether you're seeking professional advancement, personal fulfillment, or a complete life transformation, the insights and strategies ahead will serve as your roadmap. You'll gain a clearer vision of what's possible, a stronger belief in your capabilities, and actionable steps to turn your potential into reality.

Embracing the Journey

But true mastery is not a destination - it's a lifelong journey of growth and discovery. The principles in this book are not meant for passive reading; they're designed to be lived and embodied. By consistently applying these strategies and pushing beyond your comfort zone, you'll unlock new levels of success and personal fulfillment.

Your Infinite Potential

As you start this journey, remember that your potential knows no bounds. Your future is limited only by the depth of your determination and the breadth of your imagination. Greatness is not reserved for a select few; it's the birthright of every individual who dares to embrace their power and commit to their highest potential.

Maximizing Your Growth

To make the most of this transformative journey, approach this book as an interactive guide. As you read, reflect on how the concepts apply to your unique circumstances. Engage with the practical exercises and integrate the insights into your daily life. By applying these principles, you'll accelerate your growth and unlock the full value of the content.

This book has a lot of valuable information and insights. To maximize your learning and personal growth, I recommend reading through the entire book to gain a comprehensive understanding of the topics covered. After this initial read-through, reflect on the areas that resonate most strongly with your current challenges and goals. Select one specific area you feel will have the greatest impact on your life and dedicate focused time and energy to studying that section in greater depth.

Embracing Your Transformation

So take a deep breath, turn the page, and prepare to start the most transformative journey of your life. Your potential is waiting to be unleashed, and your future is ready to be shaped by the choices you make today. Let's dive in and start unlocking the incredible power within you - the power to create a life beyond your wildest dreams.

Rae A. Stonehouse

Author

COPYRIGHT

ISBNs:

Ebook: 978-1-998591-65-7

Paperback: 978-1-998591-66-4

Audiobook: 978-1-998591-67-1

SECTION ONE: ASSERTIVENESS

CHAPTER ONE: MASTER YOUR CAREER - THE POWER OF PROFESSIONAL ASSERTIVENESS

THE FOUNDATION of Career Confidence

Imagine the colleague who commands attention effortlessly in meetings or negotiates with unwavering confidence. That magnetic presence isn't magic—it's professional assertiveness in action. This skill can transform your career trajectory and professional relationships.

Understanding Professional Assertiveness

Professional assertiveness exists in the sweet spot between passive acceptance and aggressive dominance. It's your authentic voice speaking with clarity and respect, creating win-win situations in every professional interaction. When you master this balance, you naturally inspire trust and cooperation.

Core Elements of Professional Power

Self-Worth Development

Transform your professional self-image through daily achievement documentation and strength-focused reflection. Regularly articulate your professional value and engage in confidence-building practices.

Your sense of worth directly affects how others perceive and respond to you.

Communication Mastery

Elevate your communication through strategic message crafting and refined listening techniques. Align your body language with your words and practice voice modulation. Effective communication is 20% what you say and 80% how you say it.

Boundary Architecture

Design professional boundaries that protect your time and energy while maintaining positive relationships. Learn to say "no" gracefully and focus on effectively. Clear boundaries earn respect and enhance your professional effectiveness.

Professional Presence Enhancement

Voice and Body Language

Develop a commanding presence through deliberate voice and body language practices. Master the art of strategic pausing, maintain appropriate eye contact, and use purposeful gestures. Your physical presence speaks before your words do.

Strategic Action Framework

Daily Implementation

Begin each day with confidence-building practices. Set clear intentions for professional interactions. Practice assertive language and maintain boundaries consistently. End each day by reflecting on your successes and areas for improvement.

Monthly Development

Assess your growing skills regularly. Integrate feedback from trusted colleagues. Expand your professional network strategically. Develop your leadership presence intentionally.

Navigating Professional Challenges

Conflict Resolution

Transform conflicts into opportunities for growth and understanding. Focus on solutions rather than problems. Maintain professional relationships while addressing issues directly. Handled well, conflicts often lead to stronger professional bonds.

Difficult Conversations

Approach challenging discussions with preparation and purpose. Manage emotions professionally while addressing important issues. Choose timing strategically and follow up consistently.

Power Language Portfolio

Learn to express yourself with authority and grace:

- "I've analyzed this situation, and here's what I propose..."
- "Let's explore how we can achieve both objectives..."
- "Based on my experience, I recommend..."

For Boundary Setting:

- "To Ensure Quality Delivery, I Need to Focus on Current Priorities..."
- "I Can Take This on Next Week When I Can Give It Full Attention..."
- "Let's Discuss How to Align This With Our Existing Commitments..."

Professional Development Path

Immediate Implementation

Choose one assertiveness technique to practice today in a low-stakes situation. Document your experience and reflect on the outcomes. Adjust your approach based on what you learn.

Weekly Focus

Implement a morning confidence routine. Practice power poses before important meetings. Use assertive language intentionally. Document your successes and learning opportunities.

Long-term Integration

Develop your leadership skills consistently. Build your professional presence deliberately. Strengthen your network strategically. Expand your sphere of influence thoughtfully.

Action Steps: Putting Professional Assertiveness into Practice

1. **Self-Reflection:**
   - Reflect on your current level of assertiveness in your professional life
   - Identify situations where you tend to be more passive or aggressive
   - Ask yourself: What holds me back from being assertive in my career?
2. **Small Wins:**
   - Choose one assertive phrase from the Power Language Portfolio to use today
   - Practice maintaining confident body language during a brief interaction
   - Set a small boundary in your work environment, such as saying no to a non-essential task
3. **Habit Building:**
   - Implement a daily morning confidence routine, including power poses and assertive intention-setting
   - Practice using assertive language in everyday professional communication
   - Make a habit of documenting your professional achievements and successes

1. **Skill Development:**
   - Focus on enhancing your communication skills, such as eliminating qualifier words and practicing strategic pausing
   - Engage in role-playing exercises to practice assertive responses in challenging situations
   - Seek opportunities to lead discussions or present ideas in meetings

2. **Environmental Design:**
   - Create a workspace that supports your assertiveness, such as displaying confidence-boosting affirmations
   - Surround yourself with colleagues who model assertive behavior and support your growth
   - Identify and reduce environmental factors that trigger passive or aggressive responses

3. **Accountability and Support:**
   - Share your assertiveness goals with a trusted colleague or mentor
   - Join a professional development group focused on communication and leadership skills
   - Seek regular feedback from supervisors and peers on your assertiveness progress

4. **Review and Reflection:**
   - Assess your progress in building assertiveness skills at the end of each week
   - Celebrate your successes, no matter how small, and learn from any setbacks
   - Reflect on how increased assertiveness is affecting your professional relationships and career trajectory

5. **Integration and Expansion:**
   - Look for opportunities to apply assertiveness skills in new contexts, such as negotiations or conflict resolution
   - Explore how assertiveness can enhance your leadership presence and influence
   - Show how to integrate assertiveness principles into your long-term career development plan

Building professional assertiveness is a journey, not a destination. Approach these action steps with patience, self-compassion, and a commitment to consistent practice. Celebrate your progress along the way, and trust that each assertive action is strengthening your professional presence and opening doors to new opportunities.

By implementing these action steps and making assertiveness a daily practice, you'll develop the confidence and skills to navigate your career with greater ease, effectiveness, and fulfillment. Your professional transformation starts now - embrace your power and step boldly into your assertive potential.

Conclusion: Your Professional Transformation Begins Now

Professional assertiveness isn't just another career skill—it's the master key that unlocks your full professional potential. Every interaction becomes an opportunity to strengthen your assertive presence and elevate your career trajectory.

Your professional voice is unique and valuable. Your ideas deserve to be heard. Your boundaries merit respect. Starting today, commit to one small step toward more assertive communication. Whether it's speaking up in your next meeting, setting a clear boundary, or negotiating for your needs, each action builds your professional power.

The most respected professionals weren't born assertive—they developed this skill through deliberate practice and consistent application. Your journey to professional mastery starts now. Take that first bold step today, knowing that each assertive choice moves you closer to your career aspirations.

Your time to shine is here. Embrace your professional power. Your future self will thank you for starting this transformation today.

Questions to ask yourself and reflect upon:

1. What situations make you hesitate to be assertive at work?
2. How has lack of assertiveness impacted your career progress?

3. What beliefs hold you back from speaking up more confidently?
4. What specific assertiveness skills do you most need to develop?
5. How would increased assertiveness change your professional relationships?

~

CHAPTER TWO: THE POWER OF ASSERTIVENESS - TAKING CONTROL OF YOUR PERSONAL LIFE
AWAKENING YOUR INNER VOICE

REMEMBER that last time you said "yes" when your heart screamed "no"? That inner voice isn't just a whisper of doubt—it's your authentic self-yearning to be heard. Let's transform that whisper into a confident, compassionate voice that shapes your life and relationships.

The Essence of True Assertiveness

Assertiveness flows naturally when you understand its true nature. It's not about dominance or winning—it's about dancing gracefully between your needs and others' boundaries. Think of it as your personal navigation system, helping you stay true to yourself while building meaningful connections.

Building Your Assertiveness Foundation

Self-Awareness Mastery

Start each day by connecting with your authentic self. Take five minutes each morning to check in with your feelings and needs. Ask yourself: "What do I truly want today? What matters most?" Document these insights in a dedicated journal, creating a map of your inner landscape.

Communication Excellence

Transform your communication style through daily practice. Begin with mirror work—stand tall, maintain eye contact with yourself, and practice expressing your thoughts clearly. Notice your body language, tone, and energy. Record yourself speaking to fine-tune your delivery.

Boundary Brilliance

Your personal boundaries are sacred territory. Start mapping them by identifying situations where you feel drained or uncomfortable. Create clear, specific statements that express your limits. Practice delivering these statements with both firmness and grace.

Emotional Intelligence Development

Develop your emotional awareness through daily observation. Notice what triggers strong reactions in you. Practice pausing before respond-ing. Consider others' perspectives while honoring your own. This balance creates powerful, authentic connections.

Action Steps: Putting Personal Assertiveness into Practice

1. **Self-Reflection:**
   - Reflect on moments when you struggled to assert your needs or boundaries
   - Identify the thoughts and emotions that hold you back from being assertive
   - Ask yourself: "What would my life look like if I embraced my authentic voice?"
2. **Small Wins:**
   - Practice one assertive phrase in a low-stakes conversation today
   - Set a small boundary in your personal life, such as declining an invitation that doesn't align with your needs
   - Take a few minutes to celebrate your assertive victories, no matter how small

1. **Habit Building:**
   - Implement a daily morning power routine, including mindful breathing, affirmations, and intention-setting
   - Make a habit of checking in with your feelings and needs throughout the day
   - Practice expressing your thoughts and opinions clearly and confidently, even in casual conversations
2. **Skill Development:**
   - Engage in daily mirror work to improve your communication and body language
   - Role-play assertive responses to common challenging situations with a trusted friend or mentor
   - Develop your emotional intelligence by practicing active listening and empathy in your interactions
3. **Environmental Design:**
   - Create a dedicated space for your morning power routine and self-reflection
   - Surround yourself with reminders of your assertiveness goals, such as inspiring quotes or affirmations
   - Identify and reduce environmental triggers that contribute to passive or aggressive behavior
4. **Accountability and Support:**
   - Share your assertiveness journey with a trusted friend or family member
   - Join a support group or workshop focused on developing assertiveness skills
   - Seek guidance from a therapist or coach who specializes in assertiveness and personal growth
5. **Review and Reflection:**
   - Reflect on your progress and challenges in building assertiveness at the end of each week
   - Celebrate your successes and learn from any setbacks
   - Journal about how increased assertiveness is affecting your relationships and overall wellbeing

1. **Integration and Expansion:**
   - Look for opportunities to apply your assertiveness skills in various areas of your life, such as work, relationships, or personal growth
   - Explore how assertiveness can contribute to your long-term goals and values
   - Identify role models who embody healthy assertiveness and study their strategies and mindset

Personal assertiveness is a process of self-discovery and growth. Be patient and compassionate with yourself as you navigate this journey. Celebrate your progress, learn from your challenges, and trust that each assertive step is bringing you closer to a more authentic and fulfilling life.

By incorporating these action steps into your daily life and making assertiveness a consistent practice, you'll strengthen your inner voice, build healthier relationships, and create a life that aligns with your needs and values. Your journey to personal empowerment starts now - embrace your assertive potential and watch your world transform.

Conclusion: Your Journey to Personal Power

Embracing assertiveness isn't just about learning new skills, it's about uncovering the authentic power always been within you. Each time you honor your truth, set a boundary, or express your needs, you're not just changing your life; you're creating a ripple effect that inspires others to do the same.

Your journey begins with a single step—perhaps it's saying "no" to a small request or having an honest conversation with a friend. Progress isn't about perfection; it's about consistent, authentic action toward the life you deserve.

Start today. Choose one small area to practice your assertiveness. Maybe it's expressing a preference at dinner, setting a boundary with screen time, or having an honest conversation with a loved one. Each step forward builds momentum toward your transformation.

Your voice deserves to be heard. Your needs deserve to be met. Your boundaries deserve to be respected. The world is ready for your authentic self—and you're ready to shine with confidence, compassion, and unwavering self-respect.

Take that first step now. Your future self—more confident, more authentic, and more fulfilled—is already grateful for the journey you're beginning today.

Questions to ask yourself and reflect upon:

1. In what areas of your personal life do you struggle to be assertive?
2. How does your assertiveness level affect your closest relationships?
3. What fears arise when you think about being more assertive?
4. What boundaries do you need to establish or maintain?
5. How can you practice assertiveness while remaining respectful?

CHAPTER THREE: UNLEASH YOUR INNER POWER - MASTERING THE ART OF ASSERTIVENESS
THE POWER WITHIN

Have you ever felt that surge of energy when you finally speak your truth? That's your inner power waiting to be unleashed. Assertiveness isn't just a skill—it's the key to unlocking your authentic voice and creating the life you deserve.

Understanding True Assertiveness

Think of assertiveness as your internal guidance system, helping you navigate life's complexities with confidence and grace. It's the perfect balance between passive acceptance and aggressive dominance, letting you honor both your needs and others' boundaries while staying true to your core values.

The Foundation of Personal Power

Self-Awareness Development

Recognize your inherent worth by exploring your values, strengths, and unique perspectives. Start each day with intentional self-reflection, asking yourself: "What do I truly need? What matters most to me?" Document your insights and patterns in a dedicated journal.

Authentic Communication Mastery

Transform your communication style by practicing clear, confident expression. Use your natural voice while incorporating powerful language patterns. Practice scenarios in private before facing challenging conversations. Record yourself speaking to analyze and improve your delivery.

Boundary Architecture

Design your personal boundaries with intention and purpose. Start by identifying areas where you feel drained or overwhelmed. Create clear, specific statements expressing your limits. Practice delivering these statements with compassion and firmness.

Personal Leadership Development

Step into your power as a leader in your own life. Take responsibility for your choices and their outcomes. Lead by example in your relationships and professional life. Build resilience through consistent self-care and personal growth practices.

Action Steps: Putting Assertiveness Mastery into Practice

1. **Self-Reflection:**
   - Explore your core values, strengths, and unique perspectives through daily journaling
   - Identify situations where you struggle to assert your needs or maintain boundaries
   - Ask yourself: "What would my life look like if I fully embraced my inner power?"
2. **Small Wins:**
   - Practice one power pose while reciting a personal affirmation each morning
   - Engage in a brief boundary-setting exercise with a trusted friend or family member
   - Use "I feel" statements in a low-stakes conversation to express your emotions assertively

1. **Habit Building:**
    o   Implement a daily morning routine that includes gratitude, boundary review, and affirmations
    o   Make a habit of reflecting on your assertiveness successes and lessons each evening
    o   Practice using your authentic voice and powerful language patterns in everyday conversations
2. **Skill Development:**
    o   Record yourself speaking and analyze your communication style, noting areas for improvement
    o   Role-play challenging conversations and boundary-setting scenarios to build confidence
    o   Develop your emotional regulation skills through breathwork and mindfulness practices
3. **Environmental Design:**
    o   Create a dedicated space for your morning assertiveness routine and self-reflection
    o   Surround yourself with reminders of your personal power, such as inspiring quotes or images
    o   Identify and reduce environmental triggers that contribute to passive or aggressive behavior
4. **Accountability and Support:**
    o   Share your assertiveness goals with a trusted friend, family member, or mentor
    o   Join a support group or workshop focused on developing assertiveness skills
    o   Work with a coach or therapist who specializes in assertiveness and personal empowerment
5. **Review and Reflection:**
    o   Celebrate your assertiveness successes and identify key lessons at the end of each week
    o   Reflect on how increased assertiveness is affecting your relationships, career, and overall wellbeing
    o   Continuously refine your assertiveness strategies based on your experiences and insights

1. **Integration and Expansion:**
   - Apply your assertiveness skills in progressively challenging situations, such as difficult conversations or complex negotiations
   - Explore how assertiveness can enhance your leadership abilities and professional growth
   - Integrate assertiveness principles into your long-term personal development plan

Mastering assertiveness is a lifelong journey of self-discovery and growth. Approach this process with patience, self-compassion, and a commitment to consistent practice. Celebrate your progress along the way, and trust that each assertive step is strengthening your inner power and transforming your life.

By putting these action into practice steps and making assertiveness a daily practice, you'll develop confidence, resilience, and authenticity to navigate life's challenges with grace and purpose. Your journey to personal empowerment starts now - embrace your assertive potential and watch as your world expands in incredible ways.

Conclusion: Your Power Awakens

Your journey to assertiveness is a transformative adventure—one that will reshape not just how others see you, but how you see yourself. Each time you choose to speak your truth, set a healthy boundary, or honor your needs, you're not just changing your life; you're creating ripples of positive change that influence everyone around you.

The most powerful version of yourself isn't some distant future possibility—it's already within you, waiting to emerge. Every assertive choice, no matter how small, brings that powerful self closer to reality.

Start today. Choose one small area to practice your assertiveness. Maybe it's expressing a preference at lunch, setting a small boundary with a friend, or speaking up in a meeting. Each step forward builds momentum toward your transformation.

Your voice deserves to be heard. Your boundaries deserve to be honored. Your power deserves to be expressed. The world is ready for your authentic self—and you're ready to shine with confidence, grace, and unstoppable determination.

Take that first step now. Your future self is already thanking you for beginning this journey today.

Questions to ask yourself and reflect upon:

1. What are your core values and how do they guide assertive behavior?
2. How does your self-image impact your ability to be assertive?
3. What past experiences shaped your current assertiveness level?
4. What would become possible if you fully embraced your personal power?
5. How can you build confidence in expressing your needs and opinions?

SECTION ONE: CHAPTER SUMMARY - ASSERTIVENESS

CHAPTER ONE: MASTER YOUR CAREER - THE POWER OF
PROFESSIONAL ASSERTIVENESS

- Defines professional assertiveness as the balanced approach
  between passive and aggressive behavior
- Core elements: self-worth development, communication
  mastery, and boundary setting
- Emphasizes voice and body language for commanding
  presence
- Provides framework for daily and monthly skill development
- Outlines strategies for conflict resolution and difficult
  conversations
- Includes practical action steps for implementation and
  professional growth

CHAPTER TWO: THE POWER OF ASSERTIVENESS - TAKING CONTROL OF YOUR PERSONAL LIFE

- Focuses on developing authentic voice and personal boundaries
- Key components: self-awareness, communication excellence, and emotional intelligence
- Emphasizes daily practice and habit formation
- Provides concrete steps for building assertiveness in personal relationships
- Includes exercises for self-reflection and skill development
- Outlines strategies for maintaining boundaries while building connections

CHAPTER THREE: UNLEASH YOUR INNER POWER - MASTERING THE ART OF ASSERTIVENESS

- Integrates professional and personal assertivenessCore foundations: self-awareness, authentic communication, and boundary architecture
- Emphasizes personal leadership development
- Provides comprehensive action steps for assertiveness mastery
- Focuses on long-term integration and growth
- Includes reflection questions for deeper understanding

SECTION TWO: BRANDING

CHAPTER FOUR: PERSONAL BRANDING - CULTIVATING YOUR AUTHENTIC PROFESSIONAL IDENTITY

THE ESSENCE OF PERSONAL BRANDING

YOUR PERSONAL BRAND is more than a mere marketing tool; it is a powerful reflection of your unique identity, values, and contributions within your professional sphere. It encompasses the distinct qualities that set you apart, the stories that define your journey, and the indelible impact you make on those around you. When cultivated with intention and authenticity, your personal brand becomes a magnetic force, attracting opportunities and forging meaningful connections.

Building Your Authentic Foundation

Crafting a compelling personal brand begins with a deep exploration of your innermost self. Take the time to delve into the core values that guide your decisions, the passions that ignite your purpose, and the unique perspectives that shape your approach. By understanding the main elements that make you exceptional, you lay the groundwork for a brand that resonates with genuineness.

Consider the story of Sarah, a talented graphic designer who discovered that her true passion lie in creating visually stunning campaigns for environmental causes. By aligning her personal values with her professional pursuits, Sarah built a powerful brand identity that attracted like-minded clients and opportunities, letting her make a meaningful impact in her field.

Embracing Your Authentic Narrative

Your personal brand is not merely a highlight reel of achievements; it is a tapestry woven from the threads of your experiences, challenges, and triumphs. Embrace the power of storytelling to convey the depth and complexity of your professional journey. Share the transformative moments that have shaped your growth, the obstacles you have overcome, and the lessons you have learned along the way.

Take inspiration from the journey of Michael, a successful entrepreneur who openly shares his early struggles and failures as an integral part of his brand narrative. By vulnerably revealing the challenges he faced and the resilience he developed, Michael connects with his audience on a profound level, inspiring others to persevere in the face of adversity.

Navigating Cultural Influences

As you shape your personal brand, it is essential to consider the cultural context in which you operate. Our identities are intricately interconnected with the cultural norms, values, and expectations that surround us. By understanding and navigating these influences, you can create a brand that resonates with your target audience while remaining true to your authentic self.

Consider the example of Priya, a successful Indian-American entrepreneur who skillfully integrates her cultural heritage into her personal brand. By embracing her unique background and leveraging the strengths of her diverse perspective, Priya has built a thriving business that bridges cultural gaps and fosters inclusivity in her industry.

The Emotional Landscape of Branding

Building a personal brand is not merely a logical exercise; it is a deeply emotional process that requires introspection, vulnerability, and courage. As you craft your brand identity, be mindful of the emotional landscape that underlies your professional presence. Cultivate a brand that authentically reflects your passions, values, and aspirations, letting others connect with you on a profound level.

Consider the story of Emily, a passionate advocate for mental health awareness. By infusing her personal brand with the emotional depth of her own experiences and the empathy she holds for others, Emily has become a beacon of hope and support within her community. Her authentic emotional connection has let her build a loyal following and affect meaningful change.

Real-World Examples and Case Studies

To further illustrate the power of personal branding, let us explore some real-world examples and case studies of individuals who have successfully cultivated their authentic professional identities.

1. **Gary Vaynerchuk**: Gary Vaynerchuk, a renowned entrepreneur and internet personality, has built a massive personal brand by consistently delivering value, embracing authenticity, and fearlessly sharing his unique perspectives. Through his engaging content, keynote speeches, and social media presence, Gary has become a trusted voice in the business world, inspiring millions to pursue their passions and embrace their true selves.

2. **Brené Brown**: Brené Brown, a research professor and author, has built a powerful personal brand around the themes of vulnerability, courage, and authenticity. By openly sharing her own struggles and insights, Brené has connected with a global audience and sparked a conversation about the power of embracing our imperfections. Her brand has become synonymous with personal growth, resilience, and the courage to be oneself.

3. **Oprah Winfrey**: Oprah Winfrey, a media mogul and philanthropist, has cultivated one of the most recognizable personal brands in the world. Through her authentic storytelling, empathetic approach, and commitment to empowering others, Oprah has built a brand that transcends industries and touches the lives of millions. Her personal

brand is a testament to the power of authenticity, purpose, and using one's platform for positive change.

By studying these examples and drawing inspiration from their journeys, you can gain valuable insights into the art of personal branding and apply these lessons to your own professional growth.

Action Steps: Cultivating Your Personal Brand

1. **Self-Reflection**:
   - Engage in deep introspection to identify your core values, passions, and unique perspectives
   - Reflect on the experiences and challenges that have shaped your professional journey
   - Explore the cultural influences that have influenced your identity and how they can be integrated into your brand
2. **Authentic Storytelling**:
   - Craft compelling narratives that showcase your authentic journey, including triumphs and challenges
   - Infuse your brand with emotional depth and vulnerability to foster genuine connections
   - Share stories that highlight your growth, resilience, and the lessons you have learned
3. **Consistency and Coherence**:
   - Make sure your personal brand messaging is consistent across all platforms and touchpoints
   - Align your visual identity, tone of voice, and content with your core brand values
   - Regularly review and refine your brand to maintain coherence as you evolve and grow
4. **Value Creation**:
   - Focus on delivering genuine value to your audience through your expertise, insights, and unique perspectives
   - Create content, resources, and experiences that address the needs and aspirations of your target audience
   - Continuously seek opportunities to make a positive impact and contribute to your industry or community

5. **Strategic Networking**:
   - Build authentic relationships with individuals who align with your brand values and goals
   - Seek mentors, collaborators, and industry leaders who can provide guidance and support
   - Actively participate in relevant communities and events to expand your network and visibility

6. **Continuous Learning and Growth**:
   - Commit to ongoing personal and professional development to enhance your skills and knowledge
   - Stay updated on industry trends, best practices, and emerging opportunities
   - Embrace a growth mindset and view challenges as opportunities for learning and improvement

7. **Authenticity and Transparency**:
   - Remain true to your authentic self, even in the face of challenges or external pressures
   - Cultivate a brand that genuinely reflects your values, beliefs, and aspirations
   - Be transparent about your journey, acknowledging both successes and setbacks along the way

8. **Measurement and Adaptation**:
   - Regularly assess the impact and effectiveness of your personal branding efforts
   - Seek feedback from trusted mentors, colleagues, and your target audience
   - Adapt and refine your brand strategy based on insights, changing circumstances, and personal growth

By putting these actions into practice steps and committing to the ongoing cultivation of your personal brand, you will create a powerful and authentic professional identity that sets you apart and opens doors to new opportunities. Remember, your personal brand is a living, evolving entity that reflects your unique journey and the value you bring to the world.

Embrace the process of self-discovery, storytelling, and value creation as you navigate the emotional landscape of personal branding. Draw inspiration from the examples and case studies of those who have successfully built authentic and impactful brands and apply their lessons to your own journey.

Your personal brand is your platform for making a meaningful difference, forging genuine connections, and achieving your professional aspirations. By staying true to yourself, consistently delivering value, and embracing the power of your unique story, you will cultivate a brand that naturally attracts the opportunities and recognition you deserve.

Start this transformative journey with courage, authenticity, and a commitment to your own personal and professional growth. Your authentic personal brand is waiting to be discovered and shared with the world.

Questions to ask yourself and reflect upon:

1. What makes your professional story unique and compelling?
2. How well does your current brand align with your values and goals?
3. What aspects of your expertise are you not showcasing effectively?
4. How do others perceive your professional brand?
5. What specific actions would strengthen your personal brand?

CHAPTER FIVE: BUILDING A DISTINCTIVE PERSONAL BRAND IN THE DIGITAL AGE

THE EVOLUTION OF PERSONAL BRANDING

THE DIGITAL REVOLUTION has transformed personal branding from a static professional image into a dynamic, multi-platform presence. Understanding this evolution is crucial for creating lasting impact in today's interconnected world.

Digital Brand Architecture

Core Platform Strategy

Your digital presence requires strategic architecture across multiple platforms:

LinkedIn Optimization

A technology executive transformed her career trajectory through strategic LinkedIn presence:

- Daily thought leadership content
- Weekly industry analyses
- Monthly deep-dive articles
- Strategic engagement with industry leaders

Results included speaking opportunities at major conferences and a 40% increase in high-value network connections.

Platform-Specific Mastery

Twitter Brand Building

A marketing professional built significant industry influence through Twitter:

Content Strategy

- Industry insights
- Trend analysis
- Personal experiences
- Professional growth journey

Results showed 50,000 engaged followers and multiple speaking opportunities within 12 months.

Instagram Professional Presence

Case Study: Design Professional's Visual Brand

An interior designer built a thriving practice through Instagram:

Strategic Approach

- Project storytelling
- Behind-the-scenes insights
- Design philosophy sharing
- Client transformation stories

Results included a waiting list of premium clients and collaboration offers from luxury brands.

Brand Measurement and Analytics

The Impact Matrix

Modern brand measurement requires sophisticated metrics:

Quantitative Metrics

- Engagement rates across platforms
- Content performance analysis
- Network growth velocity
- Opportunity conversion rates

Case Study: Author Platform Development

A business author tracked platform growth through:

- Content resonance metrics
- Audience growth patterns
- Engagement quality analysis
- Conversion tracking

Results showed clear correlation between content types and book pre-orders.

Crisis Management Framework

The Digital Response Protocol

Effective crisis management in the digital age:

Case Study: Executive Reputation Recovery

A CEO successfully navigated a social media crisis:

Response Strategy

- Immediate acknowledgment
- Transparent communication
- Action plan implementation
- Stakeholder engagement

Results included reputation recovery within three months and strengthened stakeholder trust.

Personal Brand Innovation

The Future-Ready Framework

Building adaptable personal brands:

Innovation Elements

- Emerging platform integration
- Content format evolution
- Audience insight development
- Value proposition refinement

Case Study: Tech Influencer Evolution

A software developer built a distinctive tech education brand:

- Cross-platform presence
- Interactive content creation
- Community building
- Knowledge monetization

Results included six-figure passive income and industry thought leadership status.

Questions to ask yourself and reflect upon:

1. How effectively are you leveraging digital platforms?
2. What unique value proposition sets you apart?
3. How consistent is your brand across different channels?
4. What content could you create to demonstrate your expertise?
5. How can you make your online presence more authentic and engaging?

SECTION TWO: CHAPTER SUMMARY - BRANDING

CHAPTER FOUR: PERSONAL BRANDING - CULTIVATING YOUR AUTHENTIC PROFESSIONAL IDENTITY

- Defines personal branding as reflection of unique identity and values
- Emphasizes authentic foundation through self-exploration
- Highlights importance of storytelling and cultural influences
- Examines emotional aspects of brand building
- Provides real-world examples (Gary Vaynerchuk, Brené Brown, Oprah)
- Details action steps for brand cultivation including self-reflection, storytelling, and strategic networking

CHAPTER FIVE: BUILDING A DISTINCTIVE PERSONAL BRAND IN THE DIGITAL AGE

- Focuses on digital transformation of personal branding
- Outlines platform-specific strategies:
  - LinkedIn: Professional thought leadership

- o Twitter: Industry influence
- o Instagram: Visual brand building
- Covers brand measurement and analytics
- Provides crisis management framework
- Details future-ready innovation strategies
- Includes case studies of successful digital brand building

Key themes across both chapters:

- Authenticity in brand development
- Strategic platform utilization
- Measurement and adaptation
- Continuous evolution and growth
- Value creation and audience engagement

SECTION THREE: CAREER/JOB SEARCHING

CHAPTER SIX: THE MODERN CAREER HUNT - A COMPREHENSIVE GUIDE TO LANDING YOUR DREAM ROLE

PART ONE: FOUNDATIONS OF MODERN JOB SEARCHING

THE EVOLUTION OF JOB HUNTING

The job search landscape has transformed dramatically in recent years. Where traditional methods once dominated, digital platforms and AI-driven processes now shape how organizations find and evaluate talent. Understanding this evolution is crucial for modern job seekers. The hidden job market, increasingly accessible through digital networking, often holds the most promising opportunities. As we move through 2025-2026, emerging trends in hiring continue to favor candidates who master both traditional relationship-building and modern digital strategies.

Your Professional DNA

Beyond basic skills and experience lies your unique professional DNA – the distinctive combination of values, experiences, and perspectives that sets you apart. Begin by conducting a thorough self-assessment that considers not just your technical capabilities, but your readiness for remote work, digital collaboration, and cross-cultural engagement.

Document your industry-specific value proposition, paying particular attention to how your unique attributes align with current market demands.

Create a comprehensive skills inventory that captures both technical and soft skills, with special attention to digital competencies increasingly valued in today's workplace. Consider how your cultural preferences and work style align with different organizational environments, particularly in remote or hybrid settings.

PART TWO : DIGITAL JOB SEARCH MASTERY

MODERNPLATFORM STRATEGY

Your digital presence serves as your professional storefront. Start with LinkedIn, optimizing your profile to appeal to both human recruiters and AI screening systems. Develop a content strategy that demonstrates your expertise while engaging meaningfully with your professional community. Master the nuances of your industry's preferred platforms, whether that's GitHub for technology professionals, Behance for creatives, or specialized networks for healthcare and finance professionals.

Industry-Specific Digital Presence

Each sector demands its own unique approach to digital presence. Technology professionals should focus on demonstrating practical skills through open source contributions and technical community engagement. Creative professionals need carefully curated portfolio platforms that showcase both finished work and creative process. Finance professionals should emphasize market insight and analytical capabilities, while healthcare professionals must balance clinical expertise with technological adaptability.

PART THREE: REMOTE WORK DYNAMICS

Remote Work Readiness

The ability to excel in remote environments has become an important professional skill. Develop and document your remote work capabilities, from home office setup to digital collaboration knowledge. Show your ability to manage time effectively across time zones and maintain productivity without direct supervision. Create a narrative that showcases your virtual communication skills and ability to build relationships in digital environments.

PART FOUR: INDUSTRY-SPECIFIC GUIDANCE

Technology Sector Navigation

Success in tech requires more than coding skills. Prepare for technical assessments by developing a structured approach to problem-solving. Document your system design philosophy and maintain an active presence in technical communities. Showcase your ability to learn and adapt to new technologies while maintaining strong foundational knowledge.

Financial Services Positioning

Financial sector opportunities demand demonstration of both technical expertise and market understanding. Develop clear examples of your analytical capabilities and risk assessment approach. Prepare to discuss regulatory knowledge and compliance understanding in practical, applied contexts.

Healthcare Industry Approach

Healthcare professionals must balance clinical excellence with technological adaptability. Document your patient care philosophy while demonstrating comfort with healthcare technology. Prepare specific examples of crisis management and team collaboration in healthcare settings.

Creative Industry Strategy

Creative professionals should focus on showcasing both technical skills and innovative thinking. Document your creative process and problem-solving approach. Prepare to discuss how you balance artistic vision with practical constraints and client needs.

PART FIVE: MODERN INTERVIEW PREPARATION

The Evolution of Interviewing

Modern interviews extend far beyond traditional face-to-face conversations. Today's candidates must navigate multiple formats, from comprehensive virtual assessments to hybrid interactions. Master the nuances of each format, understanding that different skills and preparations are required for virtual versus in-person success. The key lies in maintaining authentic connection despite the medium.

Technical Excellence in Virtual Settings

Virtual interviews demand technical proficiency alongside professional expertise. Develop mastery over common interview platforms while maintaining backup plans for technical difficulties. Your virtual presence should convey the same confidence and capability as your in-person interactions. Consider lighting, background, audio quality, and body language specifically adapted for screen-based communication.

Contemporary Interview Response Frameworks

Modern interviews probe deeper than ever before, seeking evidence of adaptability, remote collaboration skills, and cultural awareness. Prepare comprehensive stories that show your capabilities across various scenarios. The STAR method (Situation, Task, Action, Result) remains relevant but must be adapted for contemporary challenges. Include examples specifically related to digital collaboration, cross-cultural communication, and remote work success.

Strategic Follow-Through

The post-interview phase requires sophisticated relationship management. Develop a system for meaningful follow-up that maintains connection without overwhelming busy professionals. Track interactions systematically while remaining genuine in your communications. Prepare thoughtful negotiation approaches that consider both traditional benefits and modern workplace considerations like remote work flexibility and professional development opportunities.

IMPLEMENTATION AND ACTION

Strategic Career Development

Transform your job search from a series of applications into a comprehensive career development campaign. Create weekly action plans that balance immediate job search activities with longer-term professional development. Maintain consistent progress through systematic tracking and regular evaluation of your efforts.

Digital Presence Building

Establish a consistent schedule for maintaining and enhancing your professional digital presence. Engage meaningfully with your professional community through thoughtful content and genuine interaction. Build relationships systematically while remaining authentic in your communications.

Industry Knowledge Development

Stay current with your industry's evolving trends and requirements. Take part in relevant professional development opportunities, whether virtual conferences, online courses, or industry webinars. Document your learning journey and share insights with your professional network.

Relationship Cultivation

Develop meaningful professional relationships through consistent, value-focused interaction. Create opportunities for genuine connection, whether through virtual coffee chats, professional group participation, or industry event engagement. Focus on building lasting relationships rather than transactional networking.

Progress Monitoring and Adjustment

Implement regular reviews of your job search strategy effectiveness. Analyze response rates, interview outcomes, and networking success. Adjust your approach based on concrete feedback and results. Celebrate progress while maintaining focus on continuous improvement.

Conclusion: Your Career Evolution

A successful modern job search combines timeless principles of professional development with mastery of contemporary tools and techniques. Your journey requires patience, persistence, and strategic adaptation. Begin today with focused action toward your professional goals, knowing that each step builds momentum toward your ideal role.

Remember that your unique combination of skills, experiences, and perspectives represents exactly what some organization needs. Approach your search with confidence, maintaining faith in your value while consistently refining your approach. The perfect role isn't just waiting – it's seeking someone with your precise capabilities.

Your career evolution begins now, guided by strategic action and supported by modern tools and techniques. Trust in your preparation, believe in your potential, and persist with purpose. Your dream career awaits, and your next step begins now.

Questions to ask yourself and reflect upon:

1. What are your non-negotiables in your next career move?
2. How well do you understand your target industry's current trends?
3. What gaps exist in your professional network?
4. How effectively are you telling your career story?
5. What unique skills or experiences set you apart from other candidates?

CHAPTER SEVEN: MASTERING PROFESSIONAL SELF-ADVOCACY IN THE DIGITAL AGE

THE EVOLUTION of Professional Visibility

The landscape of professional self-promotion has transformed dramatically in our digital era. No longer limited to traditional networking events and paper resumes, modern professionals must navigate a complex ecosystem of digital platforms, virtual relationships, and online personal branding. Success requires a sophisticated blend of authentic storytelling and strategic digital presence.

Crafting Your Professional Narrative

The Foundation: Understanding Your Value

Begin with deep self-reflection to identify your unique professional contribution. Consider the specific problems you solve, the distinctive way you approach challenges, and the measurable impact you've created in your roles. Document situations where your unique approach led to meaningful outcomes. This becomes the foundation of your professional story.

Industry-Specific Value Propositions

Technology Sector

Technology professionals must show both technical knowledge and business impact. Focus on quantifiable improvements in system performance, user experience, or business efficiency. Document your contributions to innovation, whether through patent applications, open-source contributions, or successful product launches.

Financial Services

Financial professionals should emphasize risk management capabilities and value creation. Document specific instances of portfolio performance, cost reduction initiatives, or regulatory compliance improvements. Showcase your ability to navigate complex financial environments while maintaining ethical standards.

Healthcare

Healthcare professionals must balance clinical expertise with organizational impact. Document improvements in patient outcomes, operational efficiency, and care quality metrics. Emphasize your ability to integrate new technologies while maintaining high standards of patient care.

Creative Industries

Creative professionals should showcase both artistic vision and practical results. Document how your creative solutions solved specific business challenges. Emphasize your ability to balance innovation with client needs and budget constraints.

Digital Presence Architecture

Platform Strategy

Develop a cohesive presence across key professional platforms. Your LinkedIn profile serves as your professional home base, complemented by industry-specific platforms relevant to your field. Maintain consistent messaging while adapting your tone and content to each platform's unique environment.

Content Leadership

Create valuable content that shows your expertise while serving your professional community. Share insights from your experience, analyze industry trends, and offer practical solutions to common challenges. Focus on quality over quantity, ensuring each piece adds meaningful value to professional discussions.

Remote Work Positioning

Virtual Collaboration Expertise

Document your ability to maintain productivity and build relationships in virtual environments. Showcase specific examples of successful remote project leadership, virtual team building, and digital collaboration. Emphasize your ability to maintain clear communication and strong relationships across digital channels.

Digital Communication Mastery

Develop sophisticated virtual communication skills. Master the art of engaging virtual presentations, effective digital writing, and impactful online meetings. Create a professional virtual presence that projects confidence and capability across digital platforms.

Strategic Visibility Management

Opportunity Creation

Actively generate visibility opportunities that align with your professional goals. Seek speaking engagements, writing opportunities, and project leadership roles that showcase your knowledge. Create value for your organization while building your professional reputation.

Relationship Architecture

Build meaningful professional relationships through strategic digital engagement. Take part in online professional communities, contribute to industry discussions, and maintain regular contact with key network members. Focus on creating value for others while building your professional community.

Impact Measurement and Analytics

Measuring Professional Influence

Modern self-promotion requires sophisticated tracking of your professional impact. Develop metrics that matter in your industry, whether engagement rates on thought leadership content, project success measurements, or client satisfaction scores. Create dashboards to track your visibility growth and professional reach across platforms.

Digital Footprint Analysis

Track your professional presence through both quantitative and qualitative measures. Monitor profile views, content engagement, and network growth while also assessing the quality of professional connections and opportunities generated. Document testimonials, recommendations, and specific instances where your knowledge has been recognized or sought after.

Advanced Digital Strategies

Content Ecosystem Development

Create a sustainable system for sharing your expertise. Rather than isolated posts, develop content threads that build on each other, establishing your authority in specific areas. Transform client questions into educational content, project challenges into case studies, and industry observations into trend analyses.

Professional Community Leadership

Position yourself as a community builder within your industry. Launch and moderate professional discussions, create valuable resources for peers, and help with connections between others. Your value grows exponentially when you become known not just for your expertise, but for elevating others in your field.

Virtual Event Mastery

Transform online events from passive participation to active professional development opportunities. Prepare thoroughly for virtual conferences, webinars, and networking sessions. Create meaningful engagement in chat discussions, follow up systematically with new connections, and share insights gained with your broader network.

Implementation Framework

90-Day Visibility Blueprint

First 30 Days: Foundation Building

Audit your current professional presence across all platforms. Update profiles with consistent messaging and recent achievements. Begin documenting weekly wins and insights. Schedule regular time for professional content creation and network engagement.

Days 31-60: Engagement Acceleration

Increase your content sharing frequency with emphasis on quality and value. Initiate meaningful discussions within professional groups. Reach out to one new contact daily with personalized, thoughtful messages. Begin contributing to industry publications or speaking opportunities.

Days 61-90: Authority Establishment

Launch your own professional initiative, whether a content series, virtual event, or community project. Develop collaborative opportunities with other professionals in your field. Create systems for maintaining consistent visibility while managing time effectively.

Sustainable Self-Promotion Systems

Time Management Integration

Create efficient workflows that integrate self-promotion into your daily professional routine. Set up content calendars, networking schedules, and achievement tracking systems that work within your existing commitments. Automate where possible while maintaining authenticity in your communications.

Crisis Management Preparation

Develop strategies for managing professional reputation challenges. Create response templates for common situations, establish support networks for guidance during difficult times, and maintain documentation of positive professional interactions and achievements.

Future-Proofing Your Professional Brand

Trend Adaptation

Stay ahead of evolving professional visibility trends. Monitor changes in platform algorithms, emerging communication channels, and shifting industry preferences. Adapt your strategy while maintaining consistency in your core professional message.

Skill Evolution

Continuously develop capabilities that enhance your professional presence. Master new communication tools, learn advanced content creation techniques, and stay current with industry-specific technology and trends.

Conclusion: Sustainable Professional Visibility

Professional self-promotion in the digital age requires a sophisticated balance of authenticity and strategy. Your visibility efforts should feel natural and sustainable, integrated seamlessly into your professional life rather than existing as a separate duty.

Remember that effective self-promotion serves others while advancing your own career. Each piece of content shared, connection made, or insight offered should create genuine value for your professional community. This approach ensures your visibility efforts contribute to meaningful professional relationships and opportunities.

Your expertise deserves recognition, and your insights can help others in your field. Approach self-promotion as a professional responsibility - sharing your knowledge and experience helps advance your industry while building your career. Begin putting these strategies into practice today, focusing on consistent, valuable contributions to your professional community.

The future belongs to professionals who can effectively share their knowledge while building meaningful relationships across digital platforms. Your voice matters - share it purposefully and strategically.

Questions to ask yourself and reflect upon:

1. How comfortable are you discussing your achievements?

2. What holds you back from promoting your work more actively?

3. How effectively do you communicate your value to stakeholders?

4. What opportunities for visibility are you currently missing?

5. How can you advocate for yourself while staying authentic?

CHAPTER EIGHT: MASTERING MODERN PRODUCTIVITY - ALIGNING WORK WITH PEAK PERFORMANCE

The Evolution of Productivity

The traditional nine-to-five workday is becoming obsolete. Modern professionals, especially in remote and hybrid environments, must master the art of personal productivity optimization. Understanding and leveraging your peak performance periods has become important for career success in our digital age.

Understanding Performance Rhythms

The Science of Cognitive Performance

Our brains operate on natural cycles of high and low energy, known as ultradian rhythms. These 90-120 minute cycles influence our ability to focus, create, and problem-solve. Rather than fighting these natural patterns, successful professionals learn to harness them for maximum impact.

Industry-Specific Performance Optimization

Technology Sector Performance

Software developers and technical professionals often find their deepest focus during quiet periods when interruptions are minimal.

Complex problem-solving and coding typically require extended periods of uninterrupted concentration. Many tech professionals experience peak productivity during early morning hours or late evening when digital notifications slow down.

Creative Industry Flow

Creative professionals frequently experience their best work during non-traditional hours when cognitive flexibility is highest. Many report breakthrough moments during early morning sessions or late-night creative sprints. Understanding these patterns helps structure client meetings and collaborative sessions around peak creative periods.

Financial Sector Alignment

Financial professionals must align their peak performance periods with market hours and client needs. Morning analysis and strategy development often yield the best results, while afternoon hours might be ideal for client interaction and relationship building.

Healthcare Professional Rhythms

Healthcare workers operating in shift-based environments need different strategies. Focus on maximizing performance during critical care periods while using slower periods for documentation and administrative tasks.

Remote Work Performance Optimization

Digital Environment Design

Create distinct workspace zones that signal your brain it's time for peak performance. Establish clear boundaries between focus work, collaborative sessions, and breaks. Your digital environment should support rather than hinder your natural productivity patterns.

Virtual Communication Windows

Structure your remote workday to protect your peak performance periods. Designate specific times for meetings and collaborative work, leaving your high-focus periods free for deep work. Communicate these preferences to your team to reduce interruptions during critical focus times.

Performance Tracking and Optimization

Digital Productivity Metrics

Leverage modern tools to track your productivity patterns. Track your output, energy levels, and focus quality across different times and contexts. Use this data to refine your work schedule and environment continuously.

Environment Optimization Strategy

Physical Space Enhancement

Transform your workspace into a productivity catalyst. Consider factors like natural light exposure, air quality, and ergonomic setup. Create different zones for various types of work - deep focus, creative thinking, and collaborative sessions.

Digital Space Organization

Structure your digital environment to support peak performance. Organize your tools and information for quick access during focus periods. Put systems into practice to reduce digital distractions while maintaining necessary connectivity.

Implementation Frameworks

The 90-Day Productivity Transformation

First Month: Foundation Building

Begin with conscious observation of your natural rhythms. Document your energy patterns, focusing particularly on when you naturally excel at different types of tasks. Note external factors that influence your performance - meeting schedules, environmental conditions, and social interactions. This baseline data becomes your productivity blueprint.

Second Month: Strategic Implementation

Transform your observations into structured work patterns. Reorganize your calendar to protect your peak performance periods. Establish clear boundaries around these times, communicating your new schedule to colleagues and stakeholders. Begin experimenting with different work environments and tools that support your natural rhythms.

Third Month: Refinement and Integration

Fine-tune your system based on real-world results. Adjust your schedule and environment to optimize performance further. Develop contingency plans for handling interruptions and maintaining productivity during unexpected schedule changes.

Advanced Productivity Strategies

Deep Work Protocol Development

Create personalized protocols for entering and maintaining deep focus states. Establish pre-work rituals that signal your brain it's time for intense concentration. Design recovery periods that allow for sustainable high performance without burnout.

Context-Based Work Optimization

Remote Work Mastery

Develop strategies for maintaining peak performance in virtual environments:

- Create distinct digital workspaces for different tasks
- Establish clear transitions between work modes
- Design virtual collaboration protocols that respect everyone's peak performance periods
- Implement digital boundaries that protect your focus time

Hybrid Work Performance

Master the art of maintaining productivity across different work environments:

- Align office days with collaborative tasks and meetings
- Reserve remote days for deep focus work
- Create consistent routines that translate across locations
- Develop environment-specific productivity triggers

Specific Techniques for Different Work Styles

Linear Processors

For professionals who thrive on structure and sequential processing:

- Implement time-blocking systems that align with natural energy peaks
- Create detailed task hierarchies for complex projects
- Develop systematic approaches to handling interruptions
- Design clear transition protocols between different types of work

Creative Innovators

For people who excel in non-linear thinking and creative problem-solving:

- Create flexible frameworks that allow for spontaneous insight
- Design environments that stimulate creative flow
- Develop methods for capturing and organizing random ideas
- Structure time for both focused creation and open exploration

Adaptive Multitaskers

For professionals who manage multiple concurrent priorities:

- Create systems for rapid context switching without losing momentum

- Develop clear prioritization frameworks
- Design efficient information capture and retrieval systems
- Implement regular reset points to maintain focus and direction

Sustainable Performance Systems

Energy Management

Move beyond time management to energy optimization:

- Design work patterns that respect your natural energy cycles
- Create recovery protocols for maintaining long-term performance
- Develop strategies for handling high-pressure periods without burnout
- Implement regular energy audits to maintain optimal performance

Cognitive Performance Enhancement

Optimize your mental capabilities through strategic approaches:

- Design your environment to reduce cognitive load
- Implement systems for managing information overflow
- Create protocols for maintaining mental clarity during intense work periods
- Develop practices for enhancing cognitive resilience

Future-Proofing Your Productivity

Adaptive Systems Development

Create flexible productivity systems that evolve with changing work conditions:

- Build adaptability into your routines
- Develop protocols for handling new technologies and work methods
- Create systems for continuous learning and improvement

- Implement regular productivity reviews and updates

Conclusion: Sustainable High Performance

Mastering your productivity is not about working longer hours or pushing harder. It's about understanding and working with your natural rhythms to achieve consistent, sustainable high performance. The key lies in creating personalized systems that support your unique work style while remaining flexible enough to adapt to changing circumstances.

Remember that productivity is highly individual. What works for others may not work for you. The goal is to develop a deep understanding of your own patterns and create systems that enhance rather than fight against your natural tendencies.

Start putting these strategies into practice gradually, allowing time for adaptation and refinement. Track your results, adjust your approach based on real-world feedback, and continue evolving your system as your work and circumstances change.

Your peak performance potential is waiting to be unlocked. Begin today by implementing one small change that aligns with your natural productivity patterns. Build from there, and watch as your capability for sustained high performance grows.

Questions to ask yourself and reflect upon:

1. How clear is your career vision and strategy?

2. What research have you done about potential opportunities?

3. How well-prepared are you for different interview scenarios?

4. What is your unique selling proposition?

5. How effective is your job search routine?

∾

CHAPTER NINE: MASTERING YOUR CAREER PATH - ESSENTIAL SELF-DEVELOPMENT STRATEGIES FOR PROFESSIONAL SUCCESS

TAKE the Reins of Your Career

Your career is a journey, not a destination. Today, professional success demands continuous learning, strategic thinking, and proactive self-development. By taking charge of your growth, you shape a career path that aligns with your values, leverages your strengths, and unleashes your potential.

Build Your Skill Repertoire

Expanding your skill set is the cornerstone of career development. A diverse skill portfolio positions you for evolving opportunities and roles. Focus your skill-building efforts in three key areas:

1. Technical Expertise:

- Master industry-specific tools and technologies
- Pursue relevant certifications and credentials
- Stay current with emerging trends and best practices

2. Transferable Skills:

- Strengthen your communication and collaboration abilities
- Develop your problem-solving and critical thinking skills
- Enhance your adaptability and resilience

3. Leadership Competencies:

- Cultivate your emotional intelligence
- Refine your ability to influence and inspire others
- Practice strategic thinking and decision-making

Continuously assess your skill gaps and proactively seek learning opportunities to bridge them.

Cultivate Strategic Relationships

Success is rarely a solo endeavor. Building a strong professional network is important for career growth. Focus on cultivating relationships that provide:

- Mentorship and guidance
- Opportunities for collaboration and skill-sharing
- Access to diverse perspectives and insights
- Support and encouragement during challenges

Invest time in nurturing authentic connections. Regularly engage with your network, offer value, and express gratitude for their support.

Amplify Your Professional Brand

In today's digital world, your professional reputation precedes you. Proactively shape your personal brand to showcase your unique value and expertise:

- Craft a compelling online presence that highlights your achievements and skills

- Share insights and thought leadership through content creation and public speaking
- Engage in industry conversations and contribute to relevant communities
- Seek opportunities to lead projects or initiatives that demonstrate your capabilities

Consistently communicate your brand through your actions, interactions, and digital footprint.

Embrace Stretch Opportunities

Growth often lies outside your comfort zone. Actively pursue projects and roles that challenge you to stretch your skills and expand your horizons:

- Volunteer for assignments that require you to learn and adapt quickly
- Take on leadership roles, even if you feel unprepared
- Collaborate with teams or departments outside your usual scope
- Tackle complex problems that push you to think creatively

Embracing discomfort fuels your development and opens doors to new opportunities.

Seek Feedback and Mentorship

Seeing ourselves objectively is challenging. Seek feedback from others to gain valuable insights into your strengths, blind spots, and growth areas:

- Ask for regular performance reviews from your manager
- Seek input from colleagues, clients, and mentors
- Embrace constructive criticism as an opportunity to improve
- Develop a relationship with a trusted mentor who can provide guidance and perspective

Integrating feedback into your self-development strategy accelerates your growth and enhances your self-awareness.

Action Steps: Accelerate Your Career Growth

1. Conduct a skill inventory. Identify your strengths, gaps, and priority development areas.

2. Create a learning plan. Set specific skill development goals and map out the resources and actions needed to achieve them.

3. Reach out to a potential mentor. Identify someone you admire professionally and initiate a conversation about mentorship.

4. Enhance your online presence. Update your professional profiles and share an insight or accomplishment related to your expertise.

5. Volunteer for a stretch project. Look for an opportunity to take on a challenge that pushes you outside your comfort zone.

6. Seek feedback from a trusted colleague. Ask for specific input on a recent project or interaction and identify one area for improvement.

Your career growth is a continual journey of learning, stretching, and adapting. Embrace the process, stay curious, and trust that each step is taking you closer to your professional aspirations. Your career success story starts with the actions you take today. Seize the opportunity to invest in your most valuable asset - yourself.

Questions to ask yourself and reflect upon:

1. How do you typically respond to organizational change?

2. What strategies help you adapt to new situations?

3. How effectively do you lead others through change?

4. What resistance patterns do you notice in yourself and others?

5. How can you better support team resilience during transitions?

SECTION THREE: CHAPTER SUMMARY - CAREER/JOB SEARCHING

CHAPTER 6: The Modern Career Hunt - A Comprehensive Guide to Landing Your Dream Role

- Evolution of job hunting in digital age

- Professional DNA and self-assessment

- Digital platform strategy and industry-specific presence

- Remote work readiness

- Industry-specific guidance for tech, finance, healthcare, creative sectors

- Modern interview preparation and follow-through

- Implementation framework for job search campaign

Chapter 7: Mastering Professional Self-Advocacy in the Digital Age

- Digital era professional visibility

- Crafting industry-specific value propositions

- Digital presence architecture

- Remote work positioning

- Strategic visibility management

- Impact measurement and analytics

- 90-day visibility blueprint

- Sustainable self-promotion systems

Chapter 8: Mastering Modern Productivity - Aligning Work with Peak Performance

- Understanding performance rhythms

- Industry-specific optimization

- Remote work performance

- Digital environment design

- Implementation frameworks

- Advanced productivity strategies

- Sustainable performance systems

Chapter 9: Mastering Your Career Path - Essential Self-Development Strategies

- Skill repertoire building

- Strategic relationship cultivation

- Professional brand development

- Stretch opportunity pursuit

- Feedback and mentorship

- Action steps for career growth

- Continuous learning emphasis

SECTION FOUR: CHANGE MANAGEMENT

CHAPTER TEN: MASTERING ORGANIZATIONAL CHANGE IN THE MODERN ERA

THE LANDSCAPE of change management has transformed dramatically in our digital age. Gone are the days when change followed predictable patterns and traditional models. Today's organizations must navigate a complex web of digital transformation, remote work dynamics, and rapidly shifting market conditions.

The New Change Management Paradigm

Think of modern change management as orchestrating a symphony where every section must adapt to a new piece of music while continuing to play. The digital transformation model integrates technological advancement with human elements, creating harmony between systems and people.

When a leading financial institution transformed from traditional banking to digital-first services, they discovered that success wasn't just about implementing new technology. Their triumph came from understanding that every technical change rippled through the human side of their organization. By engaging stakeholders early and maintaining strong communication channels, they achieved what many thought impossible.

Understanding Modern Resistance

Today's resistance to change looks different than it did even a few years ago. Rather than outright opposition, we often see subtle forms of disengagement - passive digital adoption, selective participation, or what I call "virtual withdrawal." A mid-sized technology company faced these exact challenges during their reorganization. Their break-through came when they stopped treating resistance as an enemy and started seeing it as valuable feedback.

Building Change-Ready Organizations

Modern organizations need to be as adaptable as water, flowing around obstacles rather than trying to break through them. This requires developing what I call "organizational adaptability DNA" - embedding change capability into every level of the organization.

Consider how a healthcare network transformed their entire operation to integrated digital care. Instead of forcing change from the top down, they built change capability throughout their organization. The result? A 40% improvement in patient satisfaction and 25% increase in operational efficiency.

Creating Sustainable Transformation

The key to lasting change lies in building sustainable systems rather than relying on short-term initiatives. An energy provider demonstrated this beautifully in their transition to sustainable operations. By focusing on long-term capability building rather than quick fixes, they achieved both environmental and operational improvements that continued to yield benefits long after the initial transformation.

Implementing Change in the Digital Age

The way we implement change has evolved dramatically. It's no longer about following a rigid playbook - it's about creating an agile framework that can adapt as quickly as your organization needs to pivot. Let me share how this works in practice.

The Power of Digital Integration

A retail chain's transformation story perfectly illustrates modern change implementation. When they decided to embrace omnichannel operations, they didn't just install new technology and hope for the best. Instead, they created what I call a "digital nervous system" - an integrated sensor network that connected every aspect of their operation.

Their store managers became digital champions, their sales staff turned into tech-savvy advisors, and their customers experienced a seamless transition between online and offline shopping. The result? A 50% surge in online sales and 35% improvement in store efficiency. But the real success wasn't in the numbers - it was in how naturally the change flowed through the organization.

Cultural Evolution: The Hidden Engine of Change

Here's something fascinating about modern change management: culture isn't just part of the change - it's the engine that drives it. A consulting firm discovered this when they embarked on their transformation journey. Instead of focusing solely on processes and systems, they invested heavily in cultural evolution.

They created what they called "culture catalysts" - team members who embodied the desired changes and helped others adapt. They didn't just tell people what to do differently; they showed them why the changes mattered and how they could personally benefit. Employee satisfaction jumped 40%, and client retention improved by 35%.

The Science of Sustainable Change

Let's talk about making change stick. An energy company's transformation offers valuable insights into sustainable change. They understood that lasting transformation isn't about big dramatic changes - it's about creating systems that naturally evolve and improve over time.

They developed what I call "change sustainability loops" - systems that continuously gather feedback, adapt processes, and reinforce positive changes. These loops helped them reduce their carbon footprint by

50% while improving operational efficiency by 30%. More importantly, these improvements continued to build on themselves long after the initial transformation period.

The Human Side of Digital Transformation

Technology might be the tool, but people are always the heart of successful change. A software company's evolution from traditional to agile operations demonstrates this perfectly. While they implemented cutting-edge systems and processes, their real breakthrough came from focusing on human connections and understanding.

They created "transformation circles" - small groups where team members could share challenges, celebrate victories, and support each other through change. This human-centered approach led to 60% faster product development and 45% higher employee engagement.

Leadership in Times of Change

Modern change management requires a new kind of leadership. We're not talking about traditional top-down direction, but rather what I call "adaptive leadership presence." A healthcare system's modernization journey illustrates this beautifully.

Their leaders became change storytellers, helping teams understand not just what needed to change, but why it mattered. They created "leadership listening posts" - regular forums where employees could share concerns and ideas. This approach turned potential resistance into valuable input for improving the transformation process.

The Future of Change Management

As we look ahead, it's clear that change management will continue to evolve. The organizations that thrive will be those that build what I call "change intelligence" - the ability to anticipate, adapt to, and lead change simultaneously.

Consider how a global manufacturing company is preparing for future transformations. They're not just implementing specific changes; they're building an organizational capacity for continuous evolution. They're creating systems that learn and adapt in real-time, leaders who facilitate rather than direct, and teams that embrace change as an opportunity rather than a challenge.

Real-World Change Management Success Stories

The Tech Startup's Transformation Tale

Let me share a fascinating example of agile change management in action. A rapidly growing tech startup faced the challenge of scaling from 50 to 500 employees while maintaining their innovative culture. Instead of traditional change management, they created what they called "growth pods."

Each pod combined veteran employees with newcomers, creating natural mentorship opportunities. They used a digital dashboard to track not just metrics, but also cultural indicators and team wellbeing. When engagement started dropping in one pod, they quickly identified the cause - communication gaps between remote and office teams - and implemented immediate solutions.

The result? They maintained a 92% employee satisfaction rate during massive growth, and their innovation output actually increased by 75%. The key was their responsive, data-driven approach to managing change.

The Retail Revolution

Here's another compelling example. A traditional retail chain with 200 stores needed to transform into an omnichannel powerhouse. Instead of forcing a one-size-fits-all approach, they created what they called "transformation laboratories" in five pilot stores.

These stores became living experiments in change management. They tested different approaches to training, customer engagement, and digital integration. Store managers became change researchers, documenting what worked and what didn't. They discovered that morning micro-training sessions were three times more effective than traditional full-day training programs.

Their most surprising finding? When they involved customers in the transformation process - actually asking for their input on changes -

customer loyalty increased by 40%. Store revenues in pilot locations grew by 28% compared to conventional stores.

Healthcare's Digital Evolution

A particularly instructive case comes from a regional healthcare network's transformation. They faced the daunting task of implementing telemedicine while maintaining quality of care. Their approach, which they called "patient-centered transformation," offers valuable lessons.

They started by creating "digital health ambassadors" - staff members who were both technically savvy and exceptionally good with patient care. These ambassadors worked one-on-one with both patients and fellow healthcare providers, creating a smooth transition to digital services.

The breakthrough came when they implemented what they called "comfort-confidence cycles" - short, repeated experiences that built both provider and patient confidence in new systems. Each cycle included:

- A small, achievable change
- Immediate feedback collection
- Quick adjustments based on feedback
- Celebration of success, no matter how small

Within six months, patient satisfaction with telemedicine services matched in-person care ratings, and provider adoption reached 94%.

Financial Services' Agile Transformation

A traditional bank's transformation into a digital-first institution provides another rich example. They developed what they called the "cascade change model," where each successful change created momentum for the next.

They began with small, visible wins - like streamlining the customer onboarding process from 45 minutes to 5 minutes. This early success created enthusiasm for bigger changes. They then introduced "transformation champions" at every branch, who became local experts and change advocates.

Their most innovative approach was creating "change stories" - regular video updates showing how specific changes were improving both employee and customer experiences. These stories made the transformation personal and relatable, leading to an 85% employee buy-in rate.

Reflection Questions for Chapter Ten: Mastering Organizational Change

Understanding Change Management

1. How has your organization's approach to change evolved in recent years?

2. What digital transformations are currently affecting your industry?

3. How well does your organization integrate technology with human needs?

4. What change management practices feel outdated in your context?

5. How do you personally adapt to organizational change?

Resistance and Adaptation

1. What subtle forms of change resistance have you observed?

2. How does your organization currently handle change resistance?

3. What valuable feedback might be hidden in resistance?

4. How could you better support others through change?

5. What makes you personally resistant to certain changes?

Building Change Capability

1. How "change-ready" is your organization?

2. What systems support or hinder adaptability?

3. How effectively does change flow through different levels?

4. What cultural elements need strengthening?

5. How could you contribute to organizational adaptability?

Digital Integration

1. How well integrated are your digital systems?

2. What gaps exist in your digital transformation?

3. How effectively do you balance technology and human needs?

4. What digital changes create the most challenge?

5. How could you better support digital adoption?

Cultural Evolution

1. How does your organizational culture support or resist change?

2. What cultural catalysts exist in your organization?

3. How effectively do you communicate change benefits?

4. What cultural shifts are needed for future success?

5. How could you influence positive cultural evolution?

Leadership and Change

1. How do your leaders approach change management?

2. What storytelling elements make change more meaningful?

3. How effectively do leaders listen to feedback?

4. What support do change leaders need?

5. How could you demonstrate change leadership?

Future Preparedness

1. How well positioned is your organization for future change?

2. What capabilities need development?

3. How can you build greater change intelligence?

4. What emerging trends might affect your organization?

5. How could you better prepare for future transformations?

Personal Development

1. What role do you play in organizational change?

2. How could you become a more effective change agent?

3. What skills would help you navigate change better?

4. How do you support others through transformation?

5. What personal changes would increase your effectiveness?

Take time to reflect on these questions within your specific context. Consider discussing them with colleagues to gain broader perspectives on change management in your organization.

CHAPTER ELEVEN: EVIDENCE-BASED TRANSFORMATION: THE SCIENCE OF PERSONAL CHANGE

UNDERSTANDING **Modern Behavioral Change**

Contemporary research reveals that sustainable personal transformation requires more than willpower or motivation. Success emerges from the intersection of behavioral science, neurology, and environmental design. This chapter explores evidence-based approaches to creating lasting change.

The Neuroscience of Habit Formation

Neural Pathway Development

Recent neurological studies demonstrate how habit formation physically restructures our brain's neural networks. Understanding this process helps design more effective change strategies:

Phase One: Initiation

The brain requires specific conditions to begin forming new neural pathways. Creating optimal circumstances for change involves:

- Dopamine optimization through small, achievable wins
- Environmental cuing that triggers desired behaviors

- Stress reduction to enhance neuroplasticity
- Social support activation for behavioral reinforcement

Case Study: Corporate Wellness Program

A Fortune 500 company revolutionized their wellness program by applying neuroscience principles. Instead of traditional incentives, they created a system based on micro-achievements and social reinforcement. Participation increased 300% within six months, with 85% of participants maintaining new health habits after one year.

Advanced Behavioral Framework

The Integrated Change Model

Modern behavioral science suggests successful change requires synchronizing multiple systems:

Identity Evolution

Transform behavior by first shifting self-perception. A technology executive successfully transitioned to entrepreneurship by gradually adopting the identity of an innovator through:

- Immersion in startup communities
- Mentorship from successful founders
- Progressive responsibility in innovation projects
- Strategic narrative development

Environmental Architecture

Context Engineering

Create environments that naturally support desired behaviors:

Physical Space Design

A healthcare organization redesigned their workspace to promote movement and collaboration. Changes included:

- Activity-based work zones

- Nature-integrated rest areas
- Social connection spaces
- Technology-free focus rooms

Results showed a 40% increase in spontaneous collaboration and a 25% reduction in reported stress levels.

Resistance Navigation

Modern Resistance Management

Contemporary approaches recognize resistance as valuable feedback rather than obstacles:

Adaptive Response Protocol

Develop systematic responses to common resistance patterns:

Case Study: Personal Fitness Transformation

An individual's successful fitness journey illustrated effective resistance management:

Initial Resistance: "No time for exercise"

Solution: Integration of movement into existing routines

Result: Sustainable 30-minute daily movement practice

Initial Resistance: "Too tired after work"

Solution: Morning micro-workouts

Result: Increased energy and consistent adherence

Implementation Systems

The Progressive Integration Model

Build sustainable change through systematic progression:

Foundation Phase

Begin with small, high-probability successes:

Case Study: Financial Behavior Change

A personal finance app successfully transformed user spending habits through:

- Micro-saving triggers
- Progressive challenge scaling
- Social accountability networks
- Celebration of small wins

Advanced Implementation Tools

Digital Transformation Framework

The Adaptive Change Matrix

Modern change requires sophisticated tracking and change systems:

Digital Integration Protocol

A healthcare startup successfully transformed patient behavior using personalized digital interventions:

Case Study: Virtual Health Transformation

The company achieved 78% adherence to new health protocols through:

- Real-time behavior tracking
- Personalized intervention timing
- AI-driven feedback loops
- Social support integration

Results showed sustained behavior change in 65% of participants after 18 months, compared to traditional programs' 15% success rate.

Organizational Change Models

The Cascade Effect Framework

Large-scale transformation requires strategic sequencing:

Case Study: Global Retail Evolution

A major retailer successfully transformed from traditional to omnichannel operations:

Phase One: Leadership Alignment

- Executive team immersion in digital retail
- Strategy development through collaborative workshops
- Clear communication of transformation vision
- Personal demonstration of new behaviors

Phase Two: Middle Management Integration

- Intensive skill development programs
- Regular feedback and change sessions
- Peer learning communities
- Recognition of early adopters

Phase Three: Frontline Implementation

- Practical training in new systems
- Daily success celebrations
- Regular troubleshooting sessions
- Continuous improvement protocols
- **Resistance Management Evolution**

The Adaptive Response System

Modern resistance management requires sophisticated understanding and response:

Case Study: Technology Company Culture Shift

A tech company successfully transformed their culture from hierarchical to collaborative:

Initial Resistance Patterns

- Senior managers protecting territory
- Middle managers feeling disempowered
- Teams struggling with new autonomy
- Cross-functional conflicts

Strategic Response Implementation

- Creation of psychological safety through transparent communication
- Development of new career advancement paths
- Implementation of skill-building programs
- Establishment of cross-functional mentoring

Results showed 85% employee engagement within 12 months, up from 45% pre-transformation.

Personal Change Architecture

The Identity Evolution Model

Sustainable personal change requires identity-level transformation:

Case Study: Career Transition Success

An executive's successful transition from finance to social impact:

Phase One: Identity Exploration

- Deep dive into personal values
- Exploration of new professional communities
- Gradual skill development
- Strategic narrative development

Phase Two: Progressive Integration

- Small project involvement
- Network building in new field

- Knowledge sharing between sectors
- Gradual responsibility increase

Phase Three: Complete Transformation

- Full transition to new role
- Integration of experience
- Development of unique value proposition
- Creation of support systems

Implementation Tools

The Digital Tracking Matrix

Modern change requires sophisticated tracking systems:

Real-time Feedback Loops

- Behavioral pattern recognition
- Intervention timing optimization
- Progress visualization
- Adjustment trigger identification

Case Study: Habit Formation Platform

A successful habit-building app achieved 72% user retention through:

- Micro-progress tracking
- Social reinforcement systems
- Personalized challenge adaptation
- Achievement celebration protocols

Conclusion: The Future of Change Management

Modern transformation requires sophisticated understanding of human behavior, technology integration, and systematic implementation. Success comes from combining proven principles with contemporary tools and approaches.

The most effective change programs recognize that transformation is both an art and a science. They combine rigorous methods with human-centered design, creating systems that work with natural behavior patterns rather than against them.

Your transformation journey begins with choosing the right framework and tools for your specific context. Start by assessing your current state, selecting appropriate tools, and implementing systematic change processes. Remember that sustainable change requires both strategic planning and adaptable execution.

Questions to ask yourself and reflect upon:

1. How specific and measurable are your current goals?

2. What makes certain goals more motivating than others?

3. How well do your goals align with your values?

4. What support systems do you need to achieve your goals?

5. How do you maintain momentum when motivation dips?

SECTION FOUR: CHAPTER SUMMARY - CHANGE MANAGEMENT

CHAPTER 10: Mastering Organizational Change in the Modern Era

- Evolution of change management in digital age

- Contemporary change management frameworks

◦ Digital Transformation Model

◦ Resistance Management

◦ Organizational Change Strategies

- Implementation tools and frameworks

◦ Digital Change Acceleration

◦ Integrated Change Matrix

◦ Adaptive Organization Model

- Case studies from various industries

- Future-ready implementation tools

Chapter 11: Evidence-Based Transformation: The Science of Personal Change

- Neuroscience of habit formation

- Advanced behavioral frameworks

∘ Integrated Change Model

∘ Environmental Architecture

∘ Resistance Navigation

- Implementation systems

∘ Progressive Integration Model

∘ Digital Transformation Framework

∘ Cascade Effect Framework

- Personal change architecture

∘ Identity Evolution Model

∘ Digital Tracking Matrix

- Case studies of successful transformations

- Future implications for change management

Key themes across both chapters:

- Integration of digital tools

- Evidence-based approaches

- Resistance management strategies

- Systematic implementation

- Real-world case studies

- Measurement and tracking

∼

SECTION FIVE: GOAL SETTING

CHAPTER TWELVE: GOAL SETTING SIMPLIFIED - A NO-NONSENSE GUIDE TO ACHIEVING YOUR DREAMS

THE PATH to Achievement

Every great accomplishment starts with a clear vision and a practical plan. While many of us have dreams and aspirations, the gap between wanting something and achieving it often feels overwhelming. Let's break down this journey into manageable steps that will transform your dreams into reality.

Understanding Effective Goal Setting

The Foundation of Achievement

Goal setting is more than just writing down wishes. It's about creating a strategic roadmap that guides your daily actions. Successful goal achievement requires clarity, commitment, and a systematic approach that aligns with your values and capabilities.

The SMART Framework Evolved

Specificity in Action

Transform vague aspirations into crystal-clear goals. Instead of "improve my career," specify secure a senior management position in digital marketing within my current company." This clarity helps your mind focus and creates a definitive target to pursue.

Measurement Mastery

Establish concrete metrics to track your progress. Create milestones that serve as checkpoints along your journey. For a fitness goal, this might mean tracking weekly workout sessions, monthly measurements, or performance benchmarks in specific exercises.

Achievability Assessment

Set challenging yet attainable goals that stretch your capabilities without breaking your spirit. Consider your current resources, skills, and time constraints. Make a realistic plan that accounts for potential obstacles and includes strategies to overcome them.

Relevance Revolution

Ensure your goals align with your core values and long-term vision. Ask yourself why each goal matters and how it fits into your larger life picture. This alignment creates intrinsic motivation that sustains you through challenges.

Time-Bound Transformation

Create urgency through specific deadlines. Break larger goals into smaller time-bound goals. For example, if your goal is to write a book, set monthly chapter completion deadlines leading to your final publication date.

Unconventional Goal Setting Strategies

Reverse Engineering

Start with your end goal and work backward to identify the steps needed to get there. This approach helps you identify potential obstacles and create a more detailed action plan. For example, if your goal is to run a marathon, start by envisioning yourself crossing the finish line and then map out the training milestones, nutrition plan, and mental preparation needed to make that vision a reality.

Passion-Driven Goals

Choose goals that ignite your passion and align with your deepest values. When you pursue goals that matter to you, motivation becomes a natural byproduct. For example, if environmental conservation is a core value, setting a goal to reduce your carbon footprint or volunteer for a local sustainability project can fuel your dedication and drive.

Experiential Goals

Focus on goals that prioritize experiences and personal growth over external measures of success. Instead of setting a goal to earn a specific salary, consider setting a goal to develop a new skill or take on a challenging project that stretches your abilities. By emphasizing personal development, you create a more rewarding and sustainable path to achievement.

Ecosystem Goals

Create goals that consider your entire life ecosystem, including your relationships, health, and personal fulfillment. A holistic approach makes sure your goals support overall well-being and balance. For example, if your career goal is to secure a promotion, consider how you can achieve this while also nurturing your family relationships and maintaining your physical and mental health.

Visionary Goals

Set goals that inspire and challenge you to think beyond your current circumstances. Dare to dream big and imagine possibilities that excite and motivate you. For example, if you've always dreamed of starting your own business, set a visionary goal to develop a groundbreaking product or service that revolutionizes your industry. Embrace the power of bold, audacious goals to fuel your motivation and creativity.

Implementation Strategy

Daily Action Framework

Develop a system for consistent daily progress:

- **Morning Planning:** Start each day reviewing your goals and identifying key actions.

- **Priority Focus:** Choose the most important task that moves you toward your goal.

- **Progress Tracking:** Document daily achievements and insights.

- **Evening Review:** Reflect on accomplishments and plan for tomorrow.

Weekly Achievement System

Create a weekly routine that maintains momentum:

- **Sunday Strategy:** Plan the week's key activities and goals.

- **Mid-Week Check-in:** Assess progress and adjust plans as needed.

- **Friday Review:** Celebrate wins and identify improvement areas.

Monthly Evolution

Establish a monthly review process:

- **Achievement Analysis:** Review progress toward larger goals.

- **Strategy Refinement:** Adjust approaches based on what's working.

- **Goal Expansion:** Set new challenges as you meet current goals.

Overcoming Obstacles

Resistance Management

Develop strategies for common challenges:

- **Procrastination Prevention:** Break tasks into smaller, manageable steps.

- **Motivation Maintenance:** Connect daily actions to your larger vision.

- **Setback Recovery:** Create bounce-back plans for inevitable obstacles.

Success Support System

Build a network that supports your goals:

• **Accountability Partners:** Find individuals who share similar ambitions.

• **Mentorship Connection:** Seek guidance from those who've met similar goals.

• **Community Engagement:** Join groups that align with your goals.

Action Steps: Putting Goal Setting into Practice

1. Self-Reflection:

◦ Identify your core values and long-term vision to ensure your goals align with your authentic self

◦ Reflect on your current resources, skills, and time constraints to set realistic and achievable goals

◦ Assess your motivation and commitment level for each goal to focus on your efforts

2. Small Wins:

◦ Choose one significant goal to focus on and apply the SMART framework to clarify your objective

◦ Break your goal down into smaller, manageable tasks and create a daily action plan

◦ Set up a tracking system to monitor your progress and maintain accountability

3. Habit Building:

◦ Establish a morning routine that includes reviewing your goals and identifying key actions for the day

◦ Make a habit of focusing on the most important task that moves you closer to your goal each day

◦ Set aside dedicated time for evening reflection to celebrate your accomplishments and plan for the next day

4. Skill Development:

◦ Identify the key skills and knowledge areas necessary to achieve your goal and create a learning plan

◦ Seek mentors, courses, or resources that can help you develop the required competencies

◦ Practice applying your new skills and knowledge consistently to reinforce your learning and progress

5. Environmental Design:

◦ Create a workspace or environment that supports your goal pursuit and reduces distractions

◦ Surround yourself with visual reminders of your goals, such as vision boards or progress trackers

◦ Curate your social environment to include supportive and like-minded individuals who encourage your growth

6. Accountability and Support:

◦ Find an accountability partner who shares similar goals or values to provide mutual support and motivation

◦ Join a community or group focused on goal achievement, personal development, or your specific area of interest

◦ Regularly share your progress, challenges, and successes with your support network to maintain momentum

7. Review and Reflection:

◦ Conduct weekly reviews to assess your progress, celebrate wins, and identify areas for improvement

◦ Adjust your strategies and plans based on your experiences and insights gained during implementation

◦ Perform a monthly review to evaluate your overall progress, set new targets, and refine your approach

8. Integration and Expansion:

◦ Look for opportunities to integrate your goal pursuit into various parts of your life, such as your work, relationships, or personal interests

◦ Explore ways to expand your goal or set new challenges as you make progress and build momentum

◦ Share your experiences, lessons learned, and achievements with others to inspire and support their own goal pursuits

Sasha's Transformation Story

Sasha had always dreamed of starting her own business, but fear and self-doubt held her back. She took control of her future by setting a SMART goal: "Launch a successful online wellness coaching business serving 10 clients within 6 months."

She broke her goal down into actionable steps, focusing on one key task each day. Sasha built a website, developed her coaching program, and started networking. She surrounded herself with motivational quotes and joined an entrepreneur support group for accountability.

As Sasha consistently worked toward her goal, she faced obstacles - technical challenges, a difficult client, moments of self-doubt. But she had developed resilience strategies, reaching out to her support network and reminding herself of her "why."

Six months later, Sasha celebrated the launch of her thriving coaching practice, serving a full roster of inspired clients. She had transformed her dream into reality through purposeful, persistent action.

Sasha's journey illustrates the power of effective goal setting. By aligning her goal with her values, breaking it into manageable steps, and maintaining focus and resilience, she achieved a deeply meaningful milestone. Her story shows that with a clear plan and consistent effort, we can all turn our aspirations into our achievements.

Goal achievement is a continuous process that requires patience, adaptability, and persistence. Embrace the challenges and setbacks as opportunities for growth and learning, and celebrate every step forward along the way.

By putting these action steps into practice and committing to consistent effort, you'll develop the mindset, skills, and habits necessary to transform your dreams into reality. Your journey to goal achievement starts now - step forward with clarity, confidence, and determination, and watch as your aspirations become your lived experiences.

Conclusion: Your Achievement Journey Begins Now

Goal achievement isn't about perfection—it's about progress. Every great accomplishment started with a single step, followed by consistent action. Your dreams are too important to leave to chance or vague planning.

Start today by choosing one meaningful goal and applying these principles. You don't need to overhaul your entire life at once. Begin with one focused goal, make your clear plan, and take that first step.

Your success is built on the actions you take today. Trust in your ability to achieve great things through systematic, intentional effort. The perfect time to begin your journey to achievement is now—take that first step today, and watch as your dreams transform into reality through focused, consistent action.

Questions to ask yourself and reflect upon:

1. How do you break down large goals into actionable steps?

2. What accountability systems work best for you?

3. How do you celebrate progress along the way?

4. What derails your goal pursuit most often?

5. How do you adjust goals when circumstances change?

CHAPTER THIRTEEN: GOAL SETTING THAT ACTUALLY WORKS - THE SMART FRAMEWORK FOR CRAFTING ACHIEVABLE OBJECTIVES

THE ACHIEVEMENT GAP

Many of us carry ambitious dreams within us—whether it's launching a business, mastering a new skill, or achieving financial independence. Yet there's often a significant gap between these aspirations and their realization. The missing link? A structured, systematic approach to goal setting that transforms vague wishes into concrete, actionable plans.

The Power of Strategic Goal Setting

Understanding SMART Goals

The SMART framework isn't just another acronym—it's a powerful tool that rewires how we think about and pursue our goals. Let's dive deep into each component and understand how to leverage it effectively.

Specificity: *The Foundation of Achievement*

Vague goals produce vague results. Instead of saying "I want to improve my fitness," define exactly what that means: "I will run a half marathon in under two hours" or "I will perform twenty consecutive pull-ups." This clarity creates a vivid target for your mind to focus on and pursue.

Examples of transforming vague goals into specific goals:

• From "save more money" to "save $12,000 for a house down payment"

• From "learn photography" to "master manual mode settings and shoot a paid wedding"

• From "start a business" to "launch an online coaching practice serving 10 clients monthly"

Measurability: Tracking Progress

What gets measured gets managed. Create concrete metrics and milestones that show your progress. Break down larger goals into quantifiable chunks you can track weekly or monthly.

For example, if your goal is to write a book:

• Weekly word count targets (5,000 words)

• Monthly chapter completion goals

• Quarterly manuscript review deadlines

• Beta reader feedback milestones

Achievability: Striking the Right Balance

Goals should stretch you without breaking you. Assess your current resources, skills, and circumstances honestly. Create challenging goals that inspire action while remaining within the realm of possibility.

Consider these factors:

• Available time and energy

• Current skill level and learning curve

• Financial resources

• Support systems

• Potential obstacles and solutions

Relevance: Aligning with Your Vision

Every goal should connect directly to your broader life vision and core values. Ask yourself:

• Why does this goal matter to me personally?

• How does it fit into my longer-term plans?

• What deeper purpose does it serve?

• Will meeting this goal bring genuine fulfillment?

Time-Bound: Creating Productive Urgency

Deadlines drive action. Set specific timeframes that create motivation without inducing panic:

• Short-term milestones (30-90 days)

• Mid-range targets (6 months)

• Long-term goals (1-3 years)

Unconventional Goal Setting Strategies

Contribution-Driven Goals

Reframe your goals in terms of the value you'll provide to others. Instead of aiming to "increase sales by 20%," consider a goal like "help 100 customers solve problem X through our product." This shift in perspective can make your goals feel more meaningful and inspiring.

Intuition-Guided Goals

Alongside rational planning, allow space for intuition and luck. Set intentions for growth and learning, then stay open to unexpected opportunities that align with your vision. Celebrate synchronicities that guide you in new directions or deepen your goals in unexpected ways.

Systems-Focused Goals

Complement your outcome-focused goals with process-oriented goals that emphasize daily habits and routines. For example, a goal like "write for 30 minutes every morning" or "have one networking conversation per week" puts the focus on consistent actions that compound over time.

Experiential Goals

Incorporate goals that focus on powerful experiences and personal growth. Expand your goal of learning a new language into "engage in a meaningful conversation with a native speaker." Achieving these experiential milestones can bring a deeper sense of fulfillment and motivation to your goal journey.

Ripple Effect Goals

Consider how your goals can create positive impact beyond yourself. A fitness goal of running a marathon could expand to "inspire five friends to start a running habit" or "raise $5,000 for a health-related charity through my race." These ripple effect goals can add depth and purpose to your individual pursuits.

Implementation Strategy

Daily Actions

Create a system for consistent progress:

1. Morning goal review and priority setting

2. Progress tracking throughout the day

3. Evening reflection and adjustment

4. Next day planning

Weekly Review Process

Maintain momentum through regular assessment:

1. Review week's achievements

2. Identify obstacles and solutions

3. Adjust strategies as needed

4. Plan next week's key actions

Monthly Evaluation

Ensure steady progress toward larger goals:

1. Measure monthly achievements

2. Update action plans

3. Celebrate progress

4. Refine approaches

Action Steps: Putting SMART Goals into Practice

1. Self-Reflection:

◦ Identify one significant goal that aligns with your core values and long-term vision

◦ Assess your current resources, skills, and circumstances honestly to ensure your goal is achievable

◦ Reflect on the deeper purpose and personal significance of your chosen goal

2. Small Wins:

◦ Apply the SMART framework to your goal, transforming it into a specific, measurable, achievable, relevant, and time-bound objective

◦ Break your SMART goal down into smaller, actionable milestones and create your first weekly action plan

◦ Set up a simple tracking system to monitor your progress and maintain accountability

3. Habit Building:

◦ Establish a morning routine that includes reviewing your goal, setting priorities, and planning your day

◦ Make a habit of tracking your progress throughout the day and documenting your achievements

◦ Set aside time for evening reflection to assess your progress, identify obstacles, and plan for the next day

4. Skill Development:

◦ Identify the key skills and knowledge areas necessary to achieve your SMART goal

◦ Make a learning plan that includes resources, mentors, and experiences to help you develop the required competencies

◦ Consistently apply and practice your new skills in your goal pursuit

5. Environmental Design:

◦ Create a workspace or environment that supports your goal achievement and reduces distractions

◦ Surround yourself with visual reminders of your SMART goal, such as progress charts or inspirational quotes

◦ Share your goal with an accountability partner or supportive community to create a positive social environment

6. Accountability and Support:

◦ Communicate your SMART goal and action plan to a trusted friend, family member, or mentor for accountability and support

◦ Join a goal-setting group or mastermind that provides guidance, motivation, and shared learning

◦ Regularly report your progress, challenges, and successes to your accountability partner or group

7. Review and Reflection:

◦ Conduct weekly reviews to assess your achievements, identify obstacles, and adjust your strategies as needed

◦ Perform a monthly evaluation to measure your progress, celebrate wins, and refine your approach based on experience

◦ Continuously update your action plans and set new targets based on your progress and insights

8. Integration and Expansion:

◦ Look for opportunities to integrate your SMART goal pursuit into various parts of your life, such as your work, relationships, or hobbies

◦ Explore ways to expand or elevate your goal as you build momentum and achieve initial milestones

◦ Share your experiences, lessons learned, and achievements with others to inspire and support their own SMART goal journeys

Achieving a SMART goal requires commitment, flexibility, and resilience. Celebrate your progress along the way, learn from setbacks, and maintain a growth mindset throughout your journey.

By implementing these action steps and consistently applying the SMART framework, you'll develop the clarity, focus, and discipline necessary to bridge the gap between your aspirations and your achievements. Your journey to goal realization begins now - take that first step with confidence, knowing you have a powerful tool and a clear path forward.

Maya's Marathon Milestone

Maya had always been an occasional jogger, but she dreamed of taking her running to the next level. Inspired by the SMART framework, she set a specific goal: "Complete my first full marathon in under 4 hours within the next 12 months."

She crafted a detailed training plan, setting weekly mileage targets and monthly race milestones. Maya joined a local running club for support and accountability. She optimized her environment, laying out her gear the night before each run and posting her progress on her fridge.

As the months went by, Maya encountered obstacles - an injury, a busy period at work, moments of self-doubt. But her SMART goal kept her focused. She adjusted her plan as needed, cross-trained during her injury, and leaned on her running community for motivation.

Twelve months later, Maya crossed the marathon finish line in 3 hours and 52 minutes, her arms raised in triumph. She had not only achieved her SMART goal, but surpassed it. The pride and satisfaction she felt were not just about the race itself, but the journey of dedication, resilience, and personal growth it represented.

Maya's marathon milestone became a powerful symbol of what she could accomplish when she set a clear intention, made a plan, and committed to consistent action. The lessons she learned on the running trail - the power of incremental progress, the importance of adaptability, and the value of a supportive community - translated to other areas of her life.

Energized by her achievement, Maya set her sights on new goals. She aimed to run a marathon in every state, using her SMART strategies to plan her training and travel. She also became a mentor for new runners, sharing her experience and encouragement with others embarking on their own fitness journeys.

Maya's story illustrates the transformative power of SMART goal setting. By turning a vague aspiration into a specific, measurable, achievable, relevant, and time-bound target, she turned her dream into reality. More than that, she discovered a new sense of confidence, resilience, and purpose that extended far beyond the finish line.

Reflection Questions:

1. What is a personal goal or dream that you've been putting off or unsure how to tackle? How could you apply the SMART framework to turn it into a concrete plan?

2. Reflect on a past achievement that required significant effort and dedication. What lessons did you learn about yourself and your capabilities through that process?

3. Who are the people in your life that could support and encourage

you as you work toward a challenging goal? How could you cultivate those relationships and build a community of accountability?

4. Envision yourself achieving a meaningful long-term goal. What would that success feel like? What impact would it have on your self-perception and future aspirations?

Remember, every big accomplishment starts with a single, SMART step. By breaking your dreams down into specific, measurable milestones and committing to consistent action, you can transform your vision into your reality.

Your SMART journey won't always be smooth or linear. You'll face obstacles, setbacks, and moments of doubt. But with a clear goal as your north star, a flexible plan as your map, and a supportive community as your traveling companions, you have everything you need to navigate the twists and turns on the path to your success.

So take a moment to reflect on the goals and dreams that light you up - the ones that both excite and scare you. Choose one to focus on and start crafting your SMART plan. Break it down into actionable steps, set milestones to celebrate your progress, and enlist the support of others who believe in your vision.

Your SMART success story is waiting to be written. You have the power to turn your aspirations into achievements, your dreams into realities. All it takes is one purposeful step, followed by another, and another.

As Maya's marathon journey shows, the true reward of a SMART goal isn't just the final outcome - it's the person you become in the process. With each challenge you overcome, each milestone you reach, you'll uncover new strengths, insights, and possibilities within yourself.

So embrace the journey of personal growth and self-discovery that SMART goal setting offers. Celebrate each victory, learn from each setback, and trust in the power of your own potential.

Your SMART future starts now. What goal will you choose to pursue first? What dream will you dare to turn into a plan? The path to your success is wide open - all you have to do is take that first SMART step.

Conclusion: Your Achievement Journey Starts Now

Effective goal setting isn't about creating an overwhelming list of goals, it's about crafting clear, actionable plans that inspire consistent progress. The SMART framework provides the structure needed to transform your aspirations into achievements.

Every significant accomplishment began with a single step followed by consistent action. Your dreams deserve more than vague wishes; they deserve a clear, strategic path to realization.

Start today by selecting one meaningful goal and applying the SMART framework. Break it down into actionable steps, create your tracking system, and take that first decisive action. Your future success is built on the decisions and actions you take today.

The perfect time to begin your journey to achievement is now. Take that first step today, and watch as your carefully crafted SMART goals transform from plans into reality through focused, consistent action.

Questions to ask yourself and reflect upon:

1. How do you break down large goals into actionable steps?

2. What accountability systems work best for you?

3. How do you celebrate progress along the way?

4. What derails your goal pursuit most often?

5. How do you adjust goals when circumstances change?

CHAPTER FOURTEEN: TRANSFORM YOUR DREAMS INTO REALITY - THE POWER OF PERSONAL ACTION LISTS

THE BRIDGE Between Dreams and Achievement

We all carry dreams within us, but the path from vision to reality often feels overwhelming. The secret to crossing this bridge? A well-crafted personal action list. Let's explore how to create and use this powerful tool to transform your aspirations into accomplishments.

Understanding Action Lists

More Than Just To-Dos

Think of your action list as a dynamic roadmap rather than a static checklist. It's a strategic tool that breaks down your grandest ambitions into manageable daily actions. This system creates clarity, maintains momentum, and builds confidence through consistent progress.

The Success Architecture

Vision Crystallization

Begin by clarifying exactly what you want to achieve. Instead of "start a business," specify "launch an online nutrition coaching practice serving 20 clients monthly by December." This clarity enables focused action and measurable progress.

Strategic Breakdown

Transform large goals into smaller, manageable parts. For example, launching a coaching business might begin with:

1. Obtaining relevant certifications

2. Creating service packages

3. Developing a marketing strategy

4. Building a website

5. Securing first clients

Priority Management

Not all actions carry equal weight. Identify the important few tasks that will create the most significant impact. Focus on these high-leverage activities first, ensuring your energy goes where it matters most.

Timeline Creation

Assign realistic yet motivating deadlines to each action item. Create a timeline that maintains steady progress without overwhelming you. Balance ambition with practicality to maintain consistent momentum.

Implementation System

Daily Action Framework

Structure your days for maximum impact:

Morning Power Hour:

- Review your action list

- Identify top priorities

- Schedule key tasks

- Prepare your workspace

Evening Review:

• Check off completed items

• Celebrate progress

• Plan tomorrow's actions

• Adjust as needed

Weekly Achievement System

Maintain momentum through regular review:

Sunday Strategy Session:

• Review week's accomplishments

• Plan next week's priorities

• Adjust timelines if needed

• Celebrate progress

Monthly Evolution

Ensure your action list stays relevant and effective:

Monthly Assessment:

• Evaluate goal progress

• Update action items

• Refine strategies

• Set new targets

Success Acceleration Techniques

Momentum Building

Create systems that maintain forward progress:

Progress Tracking:

• Keep a visible record of achievements

- Document lessons learned
- Identify patterns of success
- Adjust strategies based on results

Accountability Integration

- Build support systems that ensure follow-through:
- Share goals with trusted allies
- Schedule regular check-ins
- Join mastermind groups
- Create public commitments

Action Steps for Implementation

Start Today

1. Choose one significant goal to focus on

2. Break it down into specific action items

3. Create your tracking system

4. Schedule your first three tasks

This Week

1. Complete your first weekly review

2. Share your plan with an accountability partner

3. Track daily progress

4. Celebrate early wins

This Month

1. Conduct thorough monthly assessment

2. Refine your action list system

3. Set next month's priorities

4. Plan larger milestone celebrations

Overcoming Common Challenges

Maintaining Momentum

Address common obstacles proactively:

Motivation Dips:

- Connect actions to your bigger why
- Visualize successful completion
- Create reward systems
- Track and celebrate progress

Overwhelm Prevention:

- Focus on one key goal at a time
- Break tasks into smaller chunks
- Maintain realistic timelines
- Adjust plans as needed

Conclusion: Your Success Journey Begins Now

Every significant achievement started with a single action, followed by consistent effort. Your action list isn't just a productivity tool—it's your personal success blueprint.

Start today by selecting one meaningful goal and creating your action list. Begin with small, manageable steps that build confidence and momentum. Trust that each completed action brings you closer to your dreams.

Your success is built on the actions you take today. Don't wait for the perfect moment—create it now through decisive action. Take that first step today, and watch as your dreams transform into reality through the power of your personal action list.

Your journey to achievement begins with the next action you take. Make it count by starting your action list today. Your future self will thank you for the steps you take right now.

Questions to ask yourself and reflect upon:

Vision and Clarity

1. What dream have you been hesitating to pursue?

2. How specifically can you define your ultimate goal?

3. What would achieving this dream mean for your life?

4. What fears or doubts are holding you back?

5. How clear is your vision of success?

Action Planning

1. What's the smallest first step you could take today?

2. Which high-leverage activities would create the most impact?

3. How can you break down your goal into manageable pieces?

4. What timeline feels both challenging and achievable?

5. Which resources do you already have to support your journey?

Daily Implementation

1. How could you restructure your daily routine to support your goals?

2. What time of day are you most effective for important tasks?

3. How will you track your daily progress?

4. What might derail your daily action steps?

5. How can you prepare for potential obstacles?

Support Systems

1. Who could serve as your accountability partner?

2. What support systems do you need to build?

3. How will you celebrate small wins?

4. What communities could support your journey?

5. How will you maintain momentum during challenging times?

Progress Assessment

1. How will you measure meaningful progress?

2. What weekly review system would work best for you?

3. How will you know if your strategy needs adjustment?

4. What signs will indicate you're on the right track?

5. How will you handle setbacks or delays?

Personal Growth

1. What new skills will you need to develop?

2. How can this journey help you grow as a person?

3. What habits need to change to support your goals?

4. What beliefs might you need to challenge?

5. How will you maintain balance while pursuing your dreams?

Take a moment to reflect on these questions as you begin your journey from dreams to achievement. Remember, your answers may evolve as you progress - return to these questions regularly to reassess and realign your action steps with your vision.

~

CHAPTER FIFTEEN: FROM OVERWHELM TO MOTIVATION - BREAKING BIG GOALS INTO ACHIEVABLE STEPS

Understanding Goal Overwhelm

When facing ambitious goals, it's natural to feel paralyzed by their magnitude. Yet every significant achievement in history started with a single step, followed by consistent progress. Let's explore how to transform overwhelming aspirations into manageable actions that build unstoppable momentum.

The Psychology of Achievement

Breaking Through Mental Barriers

The human mind often struggles with large, abstract goals. By breaking them down into concrete, achievable steps, we transform intimidating challenges into manageable tasks. This process shifts our focus from overwhelming end goals to actionable daily progress.

The Milestone Mapping System

Vision Clarity

Begin by defining your ultimate goal with crystal clarity. Instead of "start a successful business," specify "build a profitable online coaching business generating $10,000 monthly revenue within 12 months." This precision creates a clear target for your planning.

Strategic Milestone Design

Work backward from your end goal to create meaningful progress markers. For a coaching business, key milestones might include:

First Quarter:

• Complete certification programs

• Develop service offerings

• Create basic marketing materials

• Secure first test client

Second Quarter:

• Launch professional website

• Establish social media presence

• Develop content strategy

• Sign three paying clients

Third Quarter:

• Implement automated systems

• Expand marketing reach

• Create more service tiers

• Reach six active clients

Fourth Quarter:

• Scale marketing efforts

- Optimize client systems

- Develop passive income streams

- Achieve revenue targets

Action Step Development

Task Breakdown Process

Transform each milestone into specific, actionable tasks. For "launch professional website":

Planning Phase:

1. Research successful competitor sites

2. Define website requirements

3. Create content outline

4. Plan user journey

Development Phase:

1. Select website platform

2. Design basic layout

3. Create core content

4. Develop service pages

Launch Phase:

1. Implement payment systems

2. Test user experience

3. Gather feedback

4. Make refinements

Implementation Framework

Daily Progress System

Create a structured approach to daily achievement:

Morning Planning:

- Review current milestone

- Select priority tasks

- Schedule specific actions

- Prepare resources

Evening Review:

- Document progress

- Celebrate completions

- Plan next day

- Address obstacles

Weekly Achievement Cycle

Maintain momentum through regular review:

Sunday Strategy:

- Assess milestone progress

- Plan weekly priorities

- Schedule key tasks

- Prepare resources

Mid-Week Check:

- Review progress

- Adjust plans

- Address challenges

- Celebrate wins

Monthly Evolution

Ensure consistent progress toward larger goals:

Monthly Assessment:

- Review milestone achievement

- Update action plans

- Refine strategies

- Set new targets

Action Steps to Begin

Immediate Actions

1. Choose one significant goal

2. Create detailed end vision

3. Map major milestones

4. Plan first week's tasks

This Week

1. Complete three specific tasks

2. Document daily progress

3. Review and adjust plans

4. Share goals with supporter

This Month

1. Achieve first mini-milestone

2. Evaluate progress systems

3. Refine action plans

4. Celebrate early wins

Overcoming Common Challenges

Maintaining Momentum

Address typical obstacles proactively:

Focus Management:

• Use time blocking

• Eliminate distractions

• Create dedicated workspace

• Track progress visually

Motivation Maintenance:

• Connect to deeper purpose

• Celebrate small wins

• Build support network

• Review progress regularly

Conclusion: Your Achievement Journey Begins Now

Every major accomplishment in history was achieved through a series of smaller steps. By breaking down your ambitious goals into manageable milestones and specific actions, you transform overwhelming challenges into achievable progress.

Start today by selecting one meaningful goal and creating your milestone map. Begin with small, confidence-building actions that create momentum. Trust that each completed task brings you closer to your ultimate vision.

Your success is built on the actions you take today. Don't wait for the perfect moment—create it now through strategic planning and consistent action. Take that first step today, and watch as your seemingly overwhelming goals transform into celebrated achievements through the power of milestone mapping.

Your journey to success begins with the next action you take. Make it count by starting your milestone map today. Your future self will thank you for the steps you take right now.

Questions to ask yourself and reflect upon:

1. What triggers overwhelm in your goal pursuit?

2. How do you maintain clarity when feeling overwhelmed?

3. What strategies help you regain motivation?

4. How do you prioritize when everything feels important?

5. What support do you need when feeling stuck?

CHAPTER SIXTEEN: CREATING A DISTRACTION-FREE ENVIRONMENT - HOW TO DESIGN THE ULTIMATE WORKSPACE FOR GOAL CRUSHING

THE FOCUS CHALLENGE

In our hyperconnected world, maintaining focus has become increasingly challenging. Yet, your ability to create and protect periods of deep work directly affects your goal achievement. Let's explore how to design a workspace that enhances focus, boosts productivity, and accelerates your progress toward important goals.

Physical Space Optimization

Sound Management

Create an audio environment that supports concentration:

Acoustic Control:

• Install sound-absorbing materials

• Use white noise machines or apps

• Consider noise-canceling headphones

• Create designated quiet zones

Visual Organization

Design a space that calms rather than clutters your mind:

Workspace Layout:

- Implement clean desk policy

- Create functional storage systems

- Maintain clear sight lines

- Remove visual distractions

Ergonomic Excellence

Support physical comfort for extended focus periods:

Comfort Optimization:

- Invest in proper seating

- Adjust monitor heights

- Create standing options

- Ensure proper lighting

Digital Distraction Management

Technology Taming

Transform your devices from distractors to supporters:

Application Control:

- Implement website blockers

- Schedule notification blackouts

- Create focused work modes

- Use productivity apps

Communication Boundaries

Establish clear protocols for availability:

Connection Management:

- Set specific check-in times

- Use status indicators

- Create response expectations

- Implement communication breaks

Motivation Enhancement

Environmental Inspiration

Incorporate elements that fuel motivation:

Visual Motivation:

- Display goal reminders

- Add inspiring artwork

- Include progress trackers

- Create vision boards

Natural Elements

Integrate nature for enhanced wellbeing:

Biophilic Design:

- Add living plants

- Maximize natural light

- Include natural materials

- Create outdoor views

Implementation Strategy

Daily Workspace Reset

Maintain your optimized environment:

Morning Setup:

1. Clear workspace

2. Arrange tools

3. Set intentions

4. Activate focus mode

Evening Cleanup:

1. Reset workspace

2. Review progress

3. Plan tomorrow

4. Close open loops

Weekly Environment Check

Regular maintenance ensures continued effectiveness:

Space Assessment:

1. Evaluate organization

2. Update inspiration elements

3. Check technology settings

4. Adjust as needed

Action Steps for Implementation

Immediate Actions

1. Conduct workspace audit

2. Remove obvious distractions

3. Install focus apps

4. Create initial organization

This Week

1. Implement sound management

2. Establish digital boundaries

3. Add inspirational elements

4. Test new setup

This Month

1. Fine-tune environment

2. Measure productivity impact

3. Adjust systems

4. Create maintenance routine

Overcoming Common Challenges

Shared Space Navigation

Solutions for non-private workspaces:

Space Management:

• Create portable focus tools

• Use visual barriers

• Establish quiet signals

• Negotiate quiet times

Technology Balance

Maintain necessary connectivity while protecting focus:

Digital Harmony:

• Create essential contacts list

• Use emergency protocols

• Schedule check-in times

• Implement focus periods

Conclusion: Your Productivity Paradise Awaits

Creating an environment that supports your goals isn't just about removing distractions—it's about designing a space that actively contributes to your success. Each element you optimize brings you closer to achieving consistent, focused productivity.

Start today by making one significant improvement to your workspace. Whether it's implementing a digital focus tool, reorganizing your desk, or adding motivational elements, act now to create your ideal achievement environment.

Your workspace is a powerful tool for goal achievement. By thoughtfully designing this space, you're setting yourself up for success. Take that first step today toward creating your ultimate productivity paradise.

Your focused future begins with the environment you create now. Make it count by acting today to optimize your workspace for achievement. Your future self will thank you for the productive sanctuary you create right now.

Questions to ask yourself and reflect upon:

1. What are your most common distractions?

2. How effectively is your workspace supporting focus?

3. What boundaries need strengthening around technology use?

4. How can you better protect your peak productivity times?

5. What environmental changes would boost your focus?

∼

CHAPTER SEVENTEEN: PROGRESS TRACKING MADE EASY - THE ESSENTIAL TOOLS FOR MONITORING YOUR GOAL JOURNEY

THE VISIBILITY CHALLENGE

Achievement requires more than just action—it demands awareness of your progress. Without clear tracking systems, it's easy to lose motivation and momentum. Let's explore how to create effective progress tracking that keeps you inspired and moving forward.

Understanding Progress Visibility

The Psychology of Progress

Our brains are wired to respond to visible progress. When we can see our advancement, even small wins trigger dopamine releases that fuel motivation. This creates a positive feedback loop of achievement and inspiration.

Comprehensive Tracking Systems

Digital Tools Integration

Leverage technology for efficient progress tracking:

Project Management Platforms:

- Task organization and milestone tracking

- Team collaboration capabilities

- Progress visualization features

- Automated reminders and updates

Analytics and Metrics:

- Key performance indicators

- Data visualization tools

- Trend analysis

- Progress comparisons

Physical Tracking Methods

Real Progress Recording

Create physical representations of your journey:

Journal Systems:

- Daily achievement logs

- Weekly progress reviews

- Monthly milestone assessments

- Lesson documentation

Visual Representations:

- Progress charts

- Achievement maps

- Milestone markers

- Success celebrations

Strategic Implementation

Daily Progress Protocol

Establish consistent tracking habits:

Morning Review:

1. Check current metrics

2. Set daily targets

3. Review upcoming milestones

4. Plan key actions

Evening Documentation:

1. Record achievements

2. Update progress markers

3. Note insights

4. Plan tomorrow

Weekly Assessment System

Maintain momentum through regular review:

Progress Analysis:

1. Compare weekly metrics

2. Identify trends

3. Adjust strategies

4. Celebrate wins

Monthly Evolution

Ensure sustained progress toward larger goals:

Comprehensive Review:

1. Evaluate monthly achievements

2. Update long-term projections

3. Refine tracking systems

4. Set new benchmarks

Customized Tracking Framework

Goal-Specific Metrics

Design tracking systems tailored to your goals:

Business Goals:

• Revenue tracking

• Client acquisition rates

• Project completion times

• Growth indicators

Personal Development:

• Skill improvement measures

• Habit formation tracking

• Learning milestones

• Achievement documentation

Action Steps for Implementation

Immediate Actions

1. Choose primary tracking tool

2. Define key metrics

3. Set up basic system

4. Record baseline data

This Week

1. Implement daily tracking

2. Complete first weekly review

3. Adjust metrics as needed

4. Share progress with accountability partner

This Month

1. Conduct comprehensive review

2. Refine tracking system

3. Celebrate early wins

4. Set next month's benchmarks

Overcoming Common Challenges

Consistency Maintenance

Address typical tracking obstacles:

System Simplification:

• Streamline tracking processes

• Automate where possible

• Remove unnecessary metrics

• Focus on key indicators

Motivation Enhancement:

• Visualize progress clearly

• Celebrate small wins

• Share achievements

• Review regularly

Technology Integration

Tool Selection

Choose and optimize tracking technologies:

Platform Assessment:

- Evaluate user-friendliness

- Consider integration needs

- Check customization options

- Review sharing capabilities

System Setup:

- Configure key metrics

- Establish automation

- Create templates

- Set up notifications

Conclusion: Your Progress Journey Begins Now

Effective progress tracking isn't about perfection, it's about awareness and momentum. Each metric you track, each achievement you document, brings you closer to your goals while maintaining motivation.

Start today by selecting one significant goal and implementing a simple tracking system. Begin with basic metrics that matter most to your success. Trust that each documented step forward builds confidence and momentum.

Your future achievements depend on your ability to see and celebrate progress. Don't wait for the perfect system—make a basic framework now and refine it as you go. Take that first step today by setting up your progress tracking system.

Your journey to achievement becomes clearer with every metric you track. Make it count by starting your progress tracking today. Your future self will thank you for the clarity and motivation you create right now.

The perfect time to begin tracking your progress is now. Act today by implementing these strategies, and watch as your goals transform from distant dreams to documented achievements.

Questions to ask yourself and reflect upon:

1. How do you currently measure progress?

2. What metrics matter most for your goals?

3. How often do you review and adjust your tracking systems?

4. What success indicators are you overlooking?

5. How can you make progress tracking more consistent?

CHAPTER EIGHTEEN: 10 ACTIONABLE STEPS TO CONQUER PROCRASTINATION AND UNLEASH YOUR PRODUCTIVITY

UNDERSTANDING **the Procrastination Puzzle**

Procrastination runs deeper than poor time management. It's a complex interplay of psychological patterns involving fear, perfectionism, and overwhelm. By understanding these underlying mechanisms, we can develop effective strategies to overcome them and unlock our productive potential.

The Psychology Behind Delay

When we procrastinate, we're often responding to deeper emotional triggers. Fear of failure, perfectionism paralysis, and success anxiety commonly drive our delay tactics. Understanding your personal triggers is the first step toward overcoming them.

Step 1: Develop Self-Awareness

Begin by observing your procrastination patterns. Notice when you delay tasks, what emotions arise, and what excuses you commonly use. This awareness becomes your foundation for change.

Step 2: Master Task Breakdown

Large projects become manageable when broken into smaller parts. Transform overwhelming tasks into bite-sized pieces that feel achievable. Create clear milestones and celebrate each completion.

Step 3: Enhance Focus

Implement structured work periods using techniques like the Pomodoro Method. Create a ritual that signals your brain it's time to focus. Eliminate distractions before they derail your progress.

Step 4: Optimize Your Environment

Your workspace significantly affects your productivity. Create an environment that supports focus and reduces distractions. Ensure everything you need is readily available.

Step 5: Transform Your Mindset

Replace self-defeating thoughts with empowering ones. Practice self-compassion while maintaining high standards. Progress, not perfection, is the goal.

Step 6: Practice Visualization

Spend time visualizing successful task completion. Feel the satisfaction of accomplishment. Let this positive emotion motivate your action.

Step 7: Build Accountability

Create systems that support your success. Find an accountability partner or join a productivity group. Regular check-ins maintain momentum.

Step 8: Establish Self-Care

Maintain your energy through proper sleep, exercise, and nutrition. A well-cared-for mind and body naturally resist procrastination.

Step 9: Celebrate Progress

Acknowledge every forward step, no matter how small. Create meaningful rewards that reinforce productive behavior.

Step 10: Cultivate Growth Mindset

View challenges as opportunities for growth. Learn from setbacks and adjust your approach.

Implementation Strategy

Today

1. Choose one delayed task

2. Break it into three manageable steps

3. Complete the first step within one hour

4. Document your success

This Week

1. Create a morning productivity ritual

2. Implement two focused work periods daily

3. Track your procrastination triggers

4. Share your progress with an accountability partner

This Month

1. Review and adjust your strategies weekly

2. Increase focused work periods gradually

3. Build consistent productive habits

4. Celebrate meaningful progress

Overcoming Resistance

Start with tiny steps to build momentum. Use the two-minute rule: if something takes less than two minutes, do it immediately. Create pre-task rituals that signal your brain it's time to focus.

Maintaining Progress

Build consistent routines that support your productivity. Track your successes and learn from setbacks. Adjust your approach based on what works best for you.

Conclusion: Your Productive Future Awaits

Overcoming procrastination isn't about achieving perfection, it's about making consistent progress through deliberate action. Each task you complete, each delay you overcome, strengthens your productivity muscle.

Begin today by choosing one small task you've been avoiding. Take immediate action, even if it's for five minutes. Momentum builds through consistent small steps.

Your success depends on the actions you take right now. Don't wait for motivation—create it through decisive action. Implement one anti-procrastination strategy today and build from there.

Your journey to peak productivity becomes clearer with every task you complete. Make today count by starting your procrastination-breaking practice. Your future self will thank you for the habits and momentum you create right now.

The perfect time to overcome procrastination is this moment. Act now by implementing these strategies, and watch as your productivity soars through consistent, focused effort. Your success story begins with the next action you take—make it count.

Questions to ask yourself and reflect upon:

1. What tasks do you most often procrastinate on?

2. What patterns precede your procrastination?

3. How do you break through procrastination when it hits?

4. What strategies have worked best for you in the past?

5. How can you better prepare for procrastination triggers?

∾

CHAPTER NINETEEN: STAYING FOCUSED AND MOTIVATED - PRACTICAL STRATEGIES FOR OVERCOMING OBSTACLES AND ACHIEVING YOUR GOALS

THE MOTIVATION CHALLENGE

We've all felt that initial surge of enthusiasm when starting something new, only to watch it fade when obstacles arise. Understanding this pattern is the first step to creating lasting motivation and meeting your goals.

Understanding Focus and Motivation

Focus and motivation aren't fixed traits—they're skills we can develop and strengthen. Like muscles, they grow stronger with consistent practice and proper technique.

The Focus Framework

Time Management Mastery

The Pomodoro Technique offers a structured approach to maintaining focus. Work in focused 25-minute blocks, followed by short breaks. This rhythm helps maintain concentration while preventing mental fatigue.

Deep Work Integration

Create designated periods for concentrated effort. Eliminate distractions, focus on single tasks, and honor your peak energy periods. Structure your environment to support deep focus.

Motivation Maintenance

Internal Drive Development

Connect daily actions to your larger purpose. Regularly review your goals and celebrate progress, no matter how small. Create clear links between current efforts and future achievements.

Achievement Architecture

Design your path to success with clear milestones. Track progress systematically and create meaningful rewards for accomplishments. Visualize success regularly to maintain inspiration.

Strategic Implementation

Daily Focus Protocol

Begin each day with a power hour: review goals, set priorities, prepare your environment, and optimize energy. End each day by documenting progress, celebrating wins, and planning for tomorrow.

Weekly Momentum Building

Evaluate progress weekly. Adjust strategies based on what's working. Celebrate achievements and plan for upcoming challenges.

Monthly Motivation Reset

Reconnect with your vision monthly. Refine strategies, acknowledge successes, and renew your inspiration. Use this time to ensure your actions align with your goals.

Obstacle Management

Challenge Solutions

Address procrastination through task breakdown and starting rituals. Create accountability systems and track progress consistently. Manage distractions by controlling your environment and setting clear boundaries.

Action Steps for Implementation

Today

1. Choose one focus technique to implement

2. Set up a simple tracking system

3. Create one environmental control

4. Schedule your first focused work session

This Week

1. Implement daily focus periods

2. Monitor effectiveness

3. Make strategy adjustments

4. Document successes

This Month

1. Review and refine your system

2. Gradually extend focus periods

3. Build consistent habits

4. Track your progress

Advanced Strategies

Flow State Cultivation

Optimize your performance by preparing your energy, environment, and mindset. Create specific triggers that signal deep focus time.

Balance challenge levels with skill development to maintain engagement.

Sustainable Success

Long-term Motivation

Maintain connection to your purpose through regular vision review. Document achievements and celebrate progress. Refine strategies based on experience and build sustainable momentum.

Conclusion: Your Focus Journey Begins Now

Maintaining focus and motivation isn't about perfection—it's about progress. Each focused session strengthens your capacity for sustained achievement.

Start today by implementing one focus strategy. Begin with short periods of concentrated effort and expand gradually. Trust that each focused action brings you closer to your goals.

Your success depends on your ability to maintain focus and motivation. Don't wait for inspiration—create it through systematic action. Take that first step today by establishing your focus routine.

Your journey to sustained achievement becomes clearer with every focused effort. Make it count by starting your focus practice today. Your future self will thank you for the habits and momentum you create right now.

The perfect time to enhance your focus and motivation is now. Act today by implementing these strategies and watch as your goals transform from distant dreams to celebrated achievements through sustained, focused effort.

Start small, stay consistent, and build progressively. Your journey to exceptional focus and motivation begins with your next action.

Here are some motivational quotes:

1. "A goal without a plan is just a wish." - Antoine de Saint-Exupery

2. "You don't have to see the whole staircase, just take the first step." - Martin Luther King Jr.

3. "The best way to predict the future is to create it." - Abraham Lincoln

4. "A year from now, you'll wish you had started today." - Karen Lamb

5. "The key to realizing a dream is to focus not on success but significance, and then even the small steps and little victories along your path will take on greater meaning." - Oprah Winfrey

6. "To accomplish great things, we must not only act, but also dream; not only plan, but also believe." - Anatole France.

Questions to ask yourself and reflect upon:

1. What helps you maintain long-term focus?

2. How do you renew motivation during challenges?

3. What distractions most often derail your focus?

4. How do you balance different priorities effectively?

5. What systems support your sustained motivation?

SECTION FIVE: CHAPTER SUMMARY - GOAL SETTING

CHAPTER 12: Goal Setting Simplified - A No-Nonsense Guide to Achieving Your Dreams

• Foundation of achievement: clarity and systematic approach

• SMART Framework: Specificity, Measurement, Achievability, Relevance, Time-bound

• Implementation strategies for daily progress

• Success story example (Sasha's transformation)

• Action steps and reflection questions

Chapter 13: Goal Setting That Actually Works - The SMART Framework

• Detailed breakdown of SMART framework components

• Unconventional goal-setting strategies

• Implementation frameworks

• Maya's marathon milestone case study

- Practical application steps

Chapter 14: Transform Your Dreams into Reality - Personal Action Lists

- Bridge between dreams and achievement

- Success architecture components

- Implementation system for daily actions

- Success acceleration techniques

- Common challenges and solutions

Chapter 15: From Overwhelm to Motivation - Breaking Big Goals

- Psychology of achievement

- Milestone mapping system

- Implementation framework

- Action step development

- Progress tracking methods

Chapter 16: Creating a Distraction-Free Environment

- Physical space optimization

- Digital distraction management

- Motivation enhancement strategies

- Implementation framework

- Solutions for common challenges

Chapter 17-19: Progress Tracking, Procrastination, and Focus

- Comprehensive tracking systems

- Anti-procrastination strategies

- Focus and motivation maintenance

- Implementation tools

- Long-term success strategies

SECTION SIX: GRATITUDE

CHAPTER TWENTY: CULTIVATING GRATITUDE - YOUR SECRET WEAPON FOR PROFESSIONAL SUCCESS

THE GRATITUDE ADVANTAGE

In today's competitive professional landscape, technical expertise alone isn't enough. The most successful professionals have discovered a powerful catalyst for career advancement: the intentional practice of gratitude. This transformative mindset can significantly elevate your professional journey.

Personal Anecdote: Linda's Gratitude Transformation

Linda, a talented marketing manager, found herself stuck in a cycle of stress and burnout. Despite her success, she struggled to find joy in her work. That changed when Linda's mentor introduced her to the power of professional gratitude.

At first, Linda was skeptical. How could something as simple as appreciation transform her career? But she committed to a daily practice of acknowledging her team's contributions, expressing gratitude to colleagues, and reflecting on her own growth.

As the weeks passed, Linda noticed a profound shift. Her relationships with coworkers deepened, her stress levels went down, and her creativity flourished. By focusing on the positive aspects of her work, Linda discovered a renewed sense of purpose and engagement.

One particularly challenging project tested Linda's newfound perspective. Instead of succumbing to frustration, she chose to appreciate her team's resilience and the opportunity for growth. This grateful approach improved team morale and led to a successful outcome that caught the attention of senior leadership.

Linda's story illustrates the transformative power of gratitude in action. By making appreciation a daily habit, she not only enhanced her own well-being but also elevated her team's performance and opened doors to new professional opportunities.

Understanding Professional Gratitude

Research consistently demonstrates that grateful professionals experience enhanced productivity, reduced stress, stronger relationships, increased job satisfaction, and improved problem-solving abilities. These benefits create a powerful foundation for career success.

Real-World Example: The Grateful Leader

Tom, a senior executive at a global technology company, attributes much of his success to his practice of professional gratitude. Each day, Tom takes time to acknowledge the efforts of his team members, express appreciation for their unique contributions, and celebrate their collective achievements.

Through this intentional practice, Tom has cultivated a loyal and engaged team that consistently outperforms expectations. His genuine appreciation has created a positive ripple effect throughout the organization, fostering a culture of recognition and collaboration.

Tom's leadership style has not gone unnoticed. His team boasts one of the highest retention rates in the company, and he is often sought for guidance by other managers. By focusing on gratitude, Tom has enhanced his own effectiveness and positioned himself as a respected and influential leader.

Strategic Gratitude Implementation

Colleague Recognition

Transform workplace relationships through meaningful appreciation. Identify specific contributions, express genuine gratitude, and share success stories. Create regular recognition moments that highlight the value others bring to your professional environment.

Meeting Enhancement

Revolutionize professional gatherings by integrating gratitude. Begin meetings with appreciation moments, acknowledge team efforts, and celebrate collective progress. Use these gatherings to reinforce positive contributions.

Position Appreciation

Develop a growth-oriented perspective toward your role. Recognize learning opportunities, document skill development, and view challenges as growth catalysts. Track your professional evolution with appreciation for each step forward.

Leadership Connection

Strengthen relationships with supervisors through thoughtful appreciation. Acknowledge specific guidance, express genuine thanks, and show how their support impacts your work. Show the value you get from their leadership.

Community Engagement

Extend professional gratitude beyond office walls. Volunteer your skills, mentor others, and share knowledge freely. Create positive impact in your professional community while building meaningful connections.

Achievement Documentation

Maintain a detailed record of progress and appreciation. Keep an accomplishment journal, document daily wins, and note received feedback. Create a real history of growth and recognition.

Cultural Development

Foster an environment where appreciation thrives. Share credit generously, create recognition programs, and build gratitude rituals into your team's culture.

Implementation Framework

Daily Practices

- Morning:

1. Review opportunities for appreciation

2. Plan recognition moments

3. Set gratitude intentions

4. Prepare specific acknowledgments

- Evening:

1. Document expressions of gratitude

2. Reflect on positive interactions

3. Plan tomorrow's recognition

4. Celebrate achievements

Weekly Integration

1. Review team contributions

2. Schedule recognition moments

3. Plan appreciation activities

4. Evaluate gratitude impact

Monthly Evolution

1. Assess practice effectiveness

2. Refine appreciation approaches

3. Expand recognition reach

4. Set new gratitude objectives

Action Steps for Implementation

Today

1. Start a gratitude journal

2. Express specific appreciation to one colleague

3. Document three professional positives

4. Plan tomorrow's recognition moment

This Week

1. Implement daily recognition practice

2. Create team appreciation ritual

3. Share success stories publicly

4. Begin tracking positive interactions

This Month

1. Develop systematic recognition approach

2. Build sustainable gratitude habits

3. Measure impact on relationships

4. Expand practice scope

Overcoming Common Challenges

Maintaining Authenticity

Focus on specific, sincere appreciation. Vary your approach while maintaining consistency. Let genuine recognition guide your practice.

Cultural Integration

Establish regular gratitude routines. Create helpful reminders and build support systems. Track progress and adjust as needed.

Conclusion: Your Gratitude Journey Begins Now

Professional gratitude isn't about empty praise—it's about creating genuine connections and recognizing real value. Each expression of appreciation builds stronger professional relationships and enhances your career trajectory.

Start today by expressing specific appreciation to one colleague. Begin with a simple, sincere acknowledgment of their contribution. Trust that each grateful interaction creates positive ripples throughout your professional life.

Your success is significantly influenced by the relationships you build and maintain. Don't wait for the perfect moment—create it through intentional gratitude. Take that first step today by implementing one gratitude practice.

Your journey to enhanced professional success becomes clearer with every expression of appreciation. Make it count by starting your gratitude practice today. Your future self will thank you for the positive professional environment and strong relationships you create right now.

The perfect time to begin cultivating professional gratitude is now. Act today by implementing these strategies and watch as your career flourishes through the power of appreciation and recognition.

Questions to ask yourself and reflect upon:

1. What are three things you're grateful for in your professional life right now?

2. How can expressing more gratitude improve your workplace relationships?

3. What barriers prevent you from practicing gratitude more consistently at work?

4. What specific actions can you take to make gratitude a daily habit?

5. How might a gratitude practice impact your leadership style and effectiveness?

CHAPTER TWENTY-ONE: THE LIFE-CHANGING POWER OF GRATITUDE - A SIMPLE PRACTICE FOR MORE JOY

Understanding Gratitude's Impact

In our achievement-driven world, we often focus on what's missing rather than what's present. This scarcity mindset leaves us feeling perpetually unfulfilled. By cultivating gratitude, we can transform our perspective and enhance our entire life experience.

Personal Anecdote: Shawn's Gratitude Journey

Shawn, a successful entrepreneur, had achieved his professional dreams but still felt a lingering sense of emptiness. In the pursuit of success, he had neglected the simple joys of life. That changed when a friend introduced him to the practice of gratitude.

At first, Shawn struggled to find things to appreciate. His mind was so accustomed to seeking problems that gratitude felt like a foreign concept. But he persisted, starting each day by listing three things he was thankful for, no matter how small.

Gradually, Shawn's perspective began to shift. He found himself noticing the beauty in everyday moments—a kindness from a stranger, a stunning sunset, a heartfelt conversation with a loved one. As his gratitude practice deepened, Shawn felt a profound sense of contentment and joy that had previously eluded him.

One particularly challenging period tested Shawn's commitment to gratitude. His business faced a significant setback, and he slipped back into negative thought patterns. But instead of giving in to despair, Shawn chose to focus on the lessons he could learn and the opportunities for growth. By maintaining his gratitude practice, even in difficult times, Shawn cultivated resilience and found the strength to overcome the obstacle.

Through gratitude, Shawn discovered a deeper sense of purpose and fulfillment. He realized that true happiness comes not from external achievements but from a grateful heart. By sharing his story and inspiring others to practice gratitude, Shawn found a new mission: spreading joy and positivity in a world that often focuses on scarcity.

Shawn's journey illustrates the life-changing power of gratitude. By making appreciation a daily practice, he transformed his perspective, found contentment in the present moment, and discovered a profound sense of purpose.

The Science of Gratitude

Research consistently shows gratitude's profound effects on both mental and physical wellbeing. Studies show increased happiness levels, reduced depression symptoms, improved stress management, and better sleep quality. Physical benefits include lower inflammation markers, decreased blood pressure, enhanced immune function, and improved heart health.

Real-World Example: The Ripple Effect of Gratitude

Emma, a teacher at a local elementary school, decided to introduce a gratitude practice to her classroom. Each day, she began by sharing something she was grateful for and encouraged her students to do the same. At first, the children were hesitant, but as the weeks passed, something remarkable happened.

The atmosphere in the classroom transformed. Students who had previously struggled with behavior issues became more cooperative and engaged. Conflicts between classmates decreased as children learned to appreciate each other's unique qualities. Academic performance improved as students developed a more positive attitude toward learning.

The impact of Emma's gratitude practice extended beyond the classroom walls. Parents reported that their children were more appreciative and helpful at home. Colleagues noticed the positive energy radiating from Emma's classroom and began incorporating gratitude into their own teaching practices.

By introducing gratitude to her students, Emma not only enhanced their individual well-being but also created a ripple effect of positivity throughout the school community. Her simple daily practice had a profound impact, demonstrating the transformative power of gratitude in action.

Gratitude Practice Framework

Daily Integration

Transform your daily experience through structured appreciation:

• Morning Ritual:

Start each day by listing three specific gratitudes, expressing appreciation, and setting a positive focus for the day ahead.

• Evening Practice:

End your day by reviewing blessings, documenting positive moments, reflecting on growth, and planning tomorrow's appreciation practice.

Deepening Your Practice

• Gratitude Journaling:

Transform simple appreciation into profound insight by writing detailed entries that connect emotionally with your experiences. Focus on specific moments, their impact on you, and your vision for the future.

• Relationship Enhancement:

Strengthen connections through expressed appreciation. Share your gratitude directly through conversation, written notes, acts of service, and shared moments of appreciation.

Action Steps for Implementation

Today

1. Begin a gratitude journal

2. Express appreciation to someone specific

3. Notice and document three positive moments

4. Create your personal morning gratitude ritual

This Week

1. Establish daily gratitude practice

2. Write three appreciation letters

3. Share your gratitude story with others

4. Document positive impacts of your practice

This Month

1. Review and refine your practice

2. Expand your appreciation scope

3. Create meaningful gratitude rituals

4. Build a supportive gratitude community

Advanced Gratitude Practices

Mindful Appreciation

Deepen your awareness through present-moment focus. Practice sensory appreciation, environmental awareness, relationship recognition, and personal growth acknowledgment.

Gratitude Expansion

Broaden your perspective by finding appreciation in challenges, recognizing growth opportunities, and considering your future legacy of gratitude.

Overcoming Practice Barriers

Building Consistency

Start small and build gradually. Create specific triggers for your practice and track your progress. Remember that consistency matters more than perfection.

Maintaining Authenticity

Focus on specific, genuine appreciation. Connect emotionally with your gratitude practice and express yourself sincerely.

Life Integration

Professional Application

Bring gratitude into your work life through colleague appreciation, achievement recognition, and growth celebration.

Personal Relationships

Enhance connections by expressing appreciation, sharing positive impact, and creating celebration moments with loved ones.

Creating Lasting Change

Habit Development

Build sustainable practices through regular reminders, varied approaches, and community support. Track your progress to maintain momentum.

Growth Mindset

View challenges through a lens of gratitude. Find learning opportunities in difficulties and celebrate progress along the way.

Conclusion: Your Gratitude Journey Begins Now

Gratitude isn't just about saying "thank you"—it's about developing a deeper appreciation for life's experiences, both challenging and joyful. Each moment of appreciation builds your capacity for joy and contentment.

Start today by noting three specific things you genuinely appreciate. Begin with simple observations and let your practice deepen naturally. Trust that each grateful thought creates positive ripples throughout your life.

Your future happiness is significantly influenced by your present perspective. Don't wait for perfect circumstances—create joy through intentional appreciation. Take that first step today by implementing one gratitude practice.

Your journey to a more fulfilled life becomes clearer with every expression of appreciation. Make it count by starting your gratitude practice today. Your future self will thank you for the positive perspective and rich relationships you create right now.

The perfect time to begin cultivating gratitude is now. Act today by implementing these strategies and watch as your life transforms through the power of appreciation and thankfulness.

Questions to ask yourself and reflect upon:

1. What moments of everyday joy do you tend to overlook?

2. How does gratitude affect your mindset and emotional wellbeing?

3. What resistance do you notice when trying to practice gratitude?

4. How can you build more gratitude into your daily routines?

5. Who are the people you're most grateful for and how can you express it?

CHAPTER TWENTY-TWO:
THE POWER OF GRATITUDE -
TRANSFORM YOUR LIFE
THROUGH THANKFULNESS

UNDERSTANDING GRATITUDE's Impact

In our endless pursuit of more, we often overlook the abundance already present in our lives. Intentional thankfulness can revolutionize your perspective and enhance every aspect of your existence.

The Neuroscience of Gratitude

Scientific research reveals gratitude's profound physiological effects on brain chemistry. When we practice gratitude, our brains release dopamine for pleasure, serotonin for improved mood, and oxytocin for deeper connection, while reducing stress-inducing cortisol.

Comprehensive Life Enhancement

Gratitude Journaling

Transform your mindset through written appreciation. Evening reflection lets you capture specific details, connect emotionally with experiences, and envision a positive future. This practice creates a tangible record of life's gifts.

Morning Mindset

Begin each day with intentional gratitude. Create an awakening ritual that includes first-thought appreciation, physical wellness acknowledgment, relationship gratitude, and recognition of daily opportunities.

Active Appreciation

Express thankfulness meaningfully through verbal expression, written notes, acts of service, and quality time. These concrete actions strengthen relationships and create lasting positive impact.

Present Moment Awareness

Develop the ability to notice life's subtle gifts. Practice mindful observation of sensory experiences, natural beauty, human connections, and daily comforts that often go unnoticed.

Service Integration

Channel gratitude into action through community engagement. Volunteer your time, perform random acts of kindness, share your skills, and give resources to those in need.

Implementation Strategy

Daily Practice

Morning Protocol:

1. Wake with intention

2. Express three specific gratitudes

3. Plan meaningful appreciation moments

4. Set a positive focus for the day

Evening Review:

1. Document daily gifts received

2. Reflect on meaningful connections

3. Plan tomorrow's gratitude practice

4. Celebrate progress made

Weekly Integration

1. Review journal entries for patterns

2. Deepen expressions of appreciation

3. Extend your gratitude reach

4. Build supportive community

Monthly Evolution

1. Assess practice impact

2. Refine your approach

3. Expand gratitude scope

4. Set inspiring new goals

Action Steps for Implementation

Today

1. Start your gratitude journal

2. Express appreciation to someone specific

3. Notice five everyday gifts

4. Create your morning ritual

This Week

1. Establish daily practice routine

2. Write three thank-you notes

3. Perform intentional acts of kindness

4. Share your gratitude story

This Month

1. Review and adjust your practice

2. Build a gratitude community

3. Create celebration rituals

4. Document positive changes

Advanced Practice Development

Relationship Enhancement

Deepen connections through shared gratitude experiences. Express specific impact, share meaningful stories, create lasting traditions, and celebrate together.

Professional Integration

Bring gratitude into your workplace through colleague appreciation, team recognition, growth acknowledgment, and success celebration.

Challenge Navigation

Building Consistency

Start small and build gradually. Create specific triggers for practice and track your progress. Remember that imperfect practice is better than no practice.

Maintaining Authenticity

Focus on deep reflection and specific expression. Maintain emotional connection and ensure sincere sharing in all gratitude practices.

Conclusion: Your Gratitude Journey Begins Now

Gratitude isn't just about saying "thank you"—it's about developing a deeper appreciation for life's rich tapestry of experiences. Each moment of thankfulness builds your capacity for joy and contentment.

Start today by noting three specific things you genuinely appreciate. Begin with simple observations and let your practice deepen naturally.

Trust that each grateful thought creates positive ripples throughout your life.

Your future happiness is significantly influenced by your present perspective. Don't wait for perfect circumstances—create joy through intentional gratitude. Take that first step today by implementing one gratitude practice.

Your journey to a more fulfilled life becomes clearer with every expression of thankfulness. Make it count by starting your gratitude practice today. Your future self will thank you for the positive perspective and rich relationships you create right now.

The perfect time to begin cultivating gratitude is now. Act today by implementing these strategies, and watch as your life transforms through the power of thankfulness and appreciation.

Questions to ask yourself and reflect upon:

1. What challenges could you reframe through a lens of gratitude?

2. How might gratitude transform your most difficult relationships?

3. What habits or practices would help you sustain a grateful mindset?

4. How does gratitude impact your resilience and ability to handle stress?

5. What are you learning about yourself through practicing gratitude?

SECTION SIX: CHAPTER SUMMARY - GRATITUDE

CHAPTER 20: Cultivating Gratitude - Your Secret Weapon for Professional Success

- The Gratitude Advantage in professional settings

- Case study: Linda's transformation through gratitude

- Strategic gratitude implementation framework

- Colleague recognition and meeting enhancement

- Action steps for workplace gratitude practice

- Solutions for maintaining authenticity

Chapter 21: The Life-Changing Power of Gratitude - A Simple Practice for More Joy

- Understanding gratitude's impact on wellbeing

- Case study: Shawn's personal gratitude journey

- Science-backed benefits of gratitude

- Emma's classroom transformation example

- Daily integration framework

- Advanced gratitude practices

Chapter 22: The Power of Gratitude - Transform Your Life Through Thankfulness

- Neuroscience of gratitude

- Comprehensive life enhancement strategies

  ◦ Gratitude journaling

  ◦ Morning mindset

  ◦ Active appreciation

  ◦ Present moment awareness

- Implementation framework

- Advanced practice development

- Challenge navigation

Key themes across chapters:

- Scientific foundation of gratitude

- Practical implementation strategies

- Personal and professional applications

- Case studies of transformation

- Overcoming common challenges

∾

SECTION SEVEN: LEADERSHIP

CHAPTER TWENTY-THREE: LEVEL UP YOUR LEADERSHIP - PRACTICAL TIPS FOR PERSONAL AND PROFESSIONAL GROWTH

The Leadership Mindset

Leadership transcends titles and positions—it's a mindset and way of being that begins with personal development. True leadership excellence starts with self-leadership, focusing on values clarification, purpose alignment, character building, and integrity maintenance.

Core Leadership Competencies

Exemplary Conduct

Your actions speak louder than words. Model the behavior you seek in others through consistent demonstration of your values, ethical decision-making, and personal accountability. When leaders embody their principles, teams naturally align with the organization's vision and goals.

Communication Mastery

Effective leadership requires exceptional communication skills. Develop your ability to listen actively, articulate clearly, and provide constructive feedback. Practice emotional intelligence in all interactions, recognizing that understanding others' perspectives is as important as expressing your own.

Adaptability Enhancement

Today's leaders must navigate constant change. Cultivate flexibility in your approach, embrace innovation, and build resilience. View challenges as opportunities for growth and lead your team through transitions with confidence and strategic thinking.

Self-Awareness Cultivation

Understanding your impact on others is important. Regularly assess your strengths and areas for improvement. Acknowledge your biases and commit to continuous personal growth. Self-aware leaders create psychologically safe environments where teams can thrive.

Professional Growth Strategy

Daily Leadership Practices

Start each day by reviewing your leadership goals and setting clear intentions. Plan key interactions and prepare your mental state. End your day by assessing your impact, documenting lessons learned, and planning improvements for tomorrow.

Weekly Development

Dedicate time each week to strengthen your leadership capacity. Review feedback received, adjust your approaches as needed, study leadership concepts, and plan specific growth activities for the coming week.

Action Steps for Implementation

Immediate Actions

Begin today by assessing your current leadership style and identifying key growth areas. Create a detailed development plan and implement daily leadership practices that align with your goals.

This Week

Focus on improving your communication skills and actively seeking feedback. Start a leadership journal to track your progress and insights. Identify one team member to mentor and schedule regular check-ins.

This Month

Develop mentorship relationships, both as mentor and mentee. Create comprehensive team development plans. Establish regular feedback systems and review mechanisms to ensure continuous improvement.

Advanced Leadership Skills

Team Empowerment

Great leaders create other leaders. Master the art of delegation, provide meaningful mentorship, and celebrate team successes. Create opportunities for team members to grow and develop their own leadership capabilities.

Innovation Leadership

Foster an environment where new ideas flourish. Encourage creative thinking and calculated risk-taking. Support the exploration and implementation of innovative solutions to challenges.

Relationship Building

Leadership effectiveness depends heavily on the strength of your professional relationships. Invest time in building trust, understanding others' perspectives, and creating collaborative partnerships across your organization.

Goal Achievement

Establish clear direction through well-defined goals and thorough resource allocation. Track progress regularly and adjust strategies as needed to ensure team success.

Conclusion: Your Leadership Journey Begins Now

Exceptional leadership isn't about perfection—it's about continuous growth and authentic connection. Each step you take in developing your leadership abilities creates positive ripples throughout your professional and personal life.

Start today by selecting one leadership quality to develop. Begin with small, consistent actions that align with your values. Trust that each leadership practice builds your capacity to inspire and influence others positively.

Your future impact is significantly influenced by the leadership habits you develop today. Don't wait for the perfect moment—create positive change through intentional leadership practice. Take that first step today by implementing one leadership development action.

Your journey to leadership excellence becomes clearer with every conscious choice and deliberate action. Make it count by starting your leadership development practice today. Your future self will thank you for the positive influence and strong relationships you create right now.

The perfect time to enhance your leadership capabilities is now. Act today by implementing these strategies, and watch as your influence grows through authentic, purposeful leadership.

Personal Motivation Boosters:

Need a little extra push? Here are some powerful motivation quotes to keep you going:

• "Believe in yourself and all that you are. Know that there is something inside you that is greater than any obstacle." - Christian D. Larson

• "Success is not final, failure is not fatal: it is the courage to continue that counts." - Winston Churchill

• "The only way to do great work is to love what you do." - Steve Jobs

• "Success is not how high you have climbed, but how you make a positive difference to the world." - Roy T. Bennett

• "Successful and unsuccessful people do not vary greatly in their abilities. They vary in their desires to reach their potential." - John Maxwell

• "Your only limit is the amount of love, courage, and strength you possess within." - Ralph Waldo Emerson

• "The only limit to our realization of tomorrow will be our doubts of today." - Franklin D. Roosevelt

• "Start where you are, use what you have, do what you can." - Arthur Ashe

• There are two types of people in this world: those who make things happen and those who watch things happen." - John Wooden

• "The only way to achieve success is to continuously work hard and never give up." - Walt Disney.

Professional Leadership: Guiding Your Team to Success

Now, let's shift our focus to the professional realm. Leadership isn't just about *you*; it's about empowering your team to achieve a shared vision. Here's how:

• **Lead With Vision:** A clear and inspiring vision is the compass of any great team. Communicate your goals and desired direction.

• **Empower, Don't Micromanage:** Encourage teamwork. Delegate tasks and provide the support to help your team to thrive.

• **Communicate, Communicate, Communicate:** Communication is important. Update everyone on open channels, and make sure regular feedback is part of the mix.

• **Foster Positivity:** A good work environment goes a long way. Encourage inclusivity, respect and make a culture of trust and teamwork.

• **Spark Innovation:** Create a space where the team can contribute their creative energies. Embrace new ideas.

• **Listen With Intent:** Really listen. Understand other's perspectives, and have open, honest dialogue.

• **Lead By Doing:** Words are just words, unless they're paired with action. Show behaviors you expect from your team.

• **Be Ready to Shift:** Times change, and great leaders adapt.

• **Set The Course:** Clear goals and direction are a must.

• **Analyze and Grow:** Evaluate your approach regularly, and be on the lookout for ways to grow.

Effective professional leadership is a mix of strong communication, a healthy work culture, and a commitment to never-ending growth and improvement.

Motivational Quotes on Professional Leadership:

Here are inspiring quotes on professional leadership:

• "A good leader takes a little more than his share of the blame, a little less than his share of the credit." - Arnold H. Glasow

• "Leadership is not about being in charge. It's about taking care of those in your charge." - Simon Sinek

• "The greatest leader is not necessarily the one who does the greatest things. He is the one that gets the people to do the greatest things." - Ronald Reagan

• "The function of leadership is to produce more leaders, not more followers." - Ralph Nader

• "The best leaders are those most interested in surrounding themselves with assistants and associates smarter than they are." - John C. Maxwell

• "A true leader has the confidence to stand alone, the courage to make tough decisions, and the compassion to listen to the needs of others." - Douglas MacArthur

• "A good leader takes a little more than his share of the blame, a little less than his share of the credit." - Arnold H. Glasow

• "The best leaders are those most interested in surrounding themselves with assistants and associates smarter than they are." - John C. Maxwell

• "Leadership is not about being in charge. It's about taking care of those in your charge." - Simon Sinek

• "A leader is one who knows the way, goes the way, and shows the way." - John C. Maxwell.

Conclusion

So, there you have it! Effective leadership is not a destination but an ongoing journey of self-improvement and a dedication to others. Implement these tips, stay motivated, and watch yourself — and your team — reach new heights! Now, go out there, lead with purpose, and make a positive impact!

Questions to ask yourself and reflect upon:

1. What defines excellent leadership in your view?

2. How do your actions align with your leadership vision?

3. What leadership skills need most development?

4. How effectively do you empower others?

5. What leadership challenges currently test you?

SECTION SEVEN: CHAPTER SUMMARY - LEADERSHIP

CHAPTER **23: The Leadership Mindset**

- Focus on self-leadership
- Values clarification
- Purpose alignment
- Character building

Core Leadership Competencies

- Exemplary conduct
- Communication mastery
- Adaptability enhancement
- Self-awareness cultivation

Professional Growth Strategy

- Daily leadership practices
- Weekly development activities
- Implementation steps:
  - Immediate actions

- Weekly focus
- Monthly development

Advanced Leadership Skills

- Team empowerment
- Innovation leadership
- Relationship building
- Goal achievement

Professional Leadership Framework

- Leading with vision
- Empowerment over micromanagement
- Communication emphasis
- Positive culture building
- Innovation fostering
- Active listening
- Leading by example
- Adaptability
- Goal setting
- Continuous growth

Key themes:

- Personal development focus
- Practical implementation strategies
- Team development emphasis
- Continuous improvement mindset
- Balance of soft and hard skills

~

SECTION EIGHT:
NETWORKING/CONNECTING

CHAPTER TWENTY-FOUR: NETWORKING IN THE DIGITAL AGE - BUILDING MEANINGFUL PROFESSIONAL CONNECTIONS
THE EVOLUTION OF PROFESSIONAL NETWORKING

THE LANDSCAPE of professional networking has transformed dramatically. While traditional face-to-face networking remains valuable, digital platforms have created unprecedented opportunities for global connection and influence. Today's successful networkers understand that authentic relationships transcend platforms, focusing instead on creating genuine value in every interaction.

Core Networking Principles

The foundation of effective networking rests on authenticity. Being genuine in all interactions creates the bedrock for lasting professional relationships. Modern networking demands a strategic approach, where clear goals guide your outreach and engagement. The most successful networkers focus on value exchange, contributing meaningful insights and assistance before seeking returns.

Digital Networking Mastery

Success in the digital age requires masterful platform optimization. Your LinkedIn profile serves as your professional storefront, while your broader social media presence reinforces your expertise. Industry-specific platforms provide targeted opportunities for meaningful connection. This digital presence must be backed by a strong content strategy, sharing thought leadership and engaging with industry trends consistently.

Building Authentic Connections

The art of connection begins with thorough research and personalized approaches. Reference shared interests and show genuine curiosity about others' work. Successful relationship nurturing demands regular, meaningful interactions and consistent follow-up. Celebrate others' successes and share relevant opportunities to strengthen these bonds.

Strategic Networking Framework

Approach networking with both short-term actions and long-term vision. Begin by auditing your current network and identifying gaps. Set clear connection goals and create an engagement plan. Over time, focus on building thought leadership and expanding your industry presence. Long-term growth comes through creating genuine influence, building strategic partnerships, and mentoring others.

Digital-Traditional Balance

Modern networking excellence requires mastery of both digital and traditional channels. While maintaining an optimized online presence and regular digital engagement is important, don't neglect the power of in-person connections through industry events, professional associations, and strategic meetings.

Networking Metrics and Goals

Measure your networking success through both qualitative and quantitative metrics. Focus on the quality of interactions, professional development opportunities, and knowledge exchange. Track network growth through meaningful new connections and engagement rates but focus on relationship depth over quantity.

Implementation Strategy

Successful networking requires daily attention through platform engagement, industry updates, and consistent outreach. Weekly focus should include content creation and relationship building, while monthly reviews allow for progress assessment and strategy adjustment.

Advanced Networking Techniques

As your network grows, focus on developing thought leadership through industry insights and professional articles. Consider speaking engagements and expert positioning opportunities. Build community through group leadership and event organization, creating collaborative projects that benefit your entire professional ecosystem.

Your Networking Evolution

Modern networking transcends simple connection-making. It's about building a professional ecosystem that supports mutual growth and creates lasting value. The most successful networkers understand that every interaction presents an opportunity to create value, share knowledge, and strengthen professional bonds.

Begin your networking evolution today by auditing your current connections and identifying three key areas for strategic growth. Create a 30-day plan focusing on strengthening these areas through targeted engagement and value creation. Remember, your network becomes your career catalyst – invest in it wisely and consistently.

The future of networking combines digital efficiency with human connection. Your success depends on mastering both elements while maintaining authenticity at every step. Start small but start today. Your professional future will be shaped by the connections you build and nurture now.

Action Items:

Immediate Actions (First 24 Hours)

Complete a network audit identifying key connections and gaps. Set up or optimize your LinkedIn profile. List three immediate networking goals. Schedule one meaningful connection activity.

First Week Priorities

Create your digital networking strategy across platforms. Develop a personalized outreach template. Schedule one industry event attendance. Set up a basic networking metrics tracking system.

Digital Presence Development

Create a content sharing calendar. Identify key industry platforms for engagement. Plan weekly thought leadership contributions. Set up professional social media tracking.

Authentication Implementation

Research five potential connections thoroughly. Draft personalized outreach messages. Create a system for tracking shared interests. Develop genuine follow-up templates.

30-Day Strategic Framework

Set specific monthly networking goals. Create weekly engagement schedules. Plan content creation timeline. Establish progress review checkpoints.

Traditional Networking Integration

Research relevant professional associations. Schedule attendance at industry events. Plan one-on-one coffee meetings. Create in-person networking goals.

Relationship Nurturing System

Develop regular check-in schedule. Create value-sharing opportunities. Plan celebration and recognition activities. Set up follow-up reminders.

Metrics and Measurement

Establish baseline networking measurements. Create qualitative assessment criteria. Set up quantitative tracking systems. Plan monthly review process.

Content Strategy Development

Plan industry insight sharing schedule. Create thought leadership topics list. Develop content creation timeline. Set engagement goals.

Community Building Focus

Identify leadership opportunities in groups. Plan collaborative project initiatives. Create community engagement schedule. Develop value-adding activities.

Professional Development Integration

Schedule speaking opportunity research. Plan expertise-sharing activities. Create mentorship connection goals. Develop professional growth timeline.

Long-term Strategy Planning

Create six-month networking roadmap. Establish quarterly review process. Set long-term connection goals. Plan strategic partnership development.

Remember to maintain authenticity throughout implementation. Start with manageable goals and gradually expand your networking activities as you build momentum and confidence.

Questions to ask yourself and reflect upon:

1. How strategic is your networking approach?
2. What value do you bring to your professional relationships?
3. How effectively do you maintain connections?
4. What networking opportunities are you missing?
5. How can you make networking more authentic?

~

CHAPTER TWENTY-FIVE: THE ART OF CONNECTION - MASTERING PERSONAL COMMUNICATION IN A DIGITAL AGE

WHEN SCREENS OFTEN SEPARATE US, the ability to connect authentically has never been more valuable. As Peter Drucker wisely noted, "The most important thing in communication is hearing what isn't said." This profound insight sets the stage for our journey into mastering personal communication.

The Foundation: Active Listening

Let's be honest – most of us aren't listening; we're waiting for our turn to speak. The anonymous wisdom rings true: "The biggest communication problem is we do not listen to understand. We listen to reply." Breaking this habit is your first step toward communication mastery.

Active listening isn't just about hearing words; it's about being fully present. Put away your phone, maintain eye contact, and lean into conversations with genuine curiosity. As Brian Tracy reminds us, "The quality of your communication directly affects the quality of your relationships and the results you get."

Beyond Words: The Power of Nonverbal Communication

Your body speaks volumes before you utter a word. Your posture, facial expressions, and even the energy you bring into a room shape how others receive your message. Remember Jim Rohn's perspective: "Effective communication is 20% what you know and 80% how you feel about what you know."

The Emotional Intelligence Factor

Managing your emotions isn't just about keeping cool – it's about creating space for authentic connection. Practice self-awareness and recognize when stress might be affecting your communication style. As L.R. Knost beautifully puts it, "Clear communication requires a clear mind and a compassionate heart."

Industry-Specific Connection Strategies - A Professional's Guide

Technology and Innovation Sector

The tech industry thrives on continuous learning and collaborative innovation. Success in this space requires engagement with technical communities through meaningful open-source contributions. Regular participation in hackathons and tech meetups builds both skills and connections. Developer forums and platforms like GitHub become your digital business card, showcasing your expertise through code rather than conversation.

Creative Industries and Design

Creative professionals must master the art of visual storytelling through their portfolio. Beyond showcasing work, building a creative community requires consistent engagement in industry events and festivals. Collaborative projects serve dual purposes - expanding your portfolio while strengthening professional relationships. Digital platforms like Behance and Dribbble become essential networking spaces where work speaks louder than words.

Business and Financial Services

Financial sector networking centers on credibility and expertise. Professional association involvement opens doors to decision-makers, while industry conferences provide platforms for thought leadership. Investment community networking requires a nuanced approach - focus on building trust through consistent value delivery. Business roundtables offer intimate settings for meaningful relationship development with industry leaders.

Healthcare and Medical Services

Medical professionals face unique networking challenges, balancing patient care with professional growth. Medical conferences serve as crucial connection points for staying current with research while building collaborative relationships. Healthcare associations provide structured networking opportunities, while research collaborations often lead to lasting professional partnerships. Professional development events offer focused opportunities for specialty-specific networking.

Education and Academia

Academic networking requires a blend of traditional scholarship and modern connection strategies. Educational forums and research networks provide platforms for sharing insights and building collaborative relationships. Professional learning communities offer ongoing support and development opportunities. Academic conferences remain central to building reputation and relationships in educational circles.

Cross-Industry Integration

Modern professionals often work across industry boundaries. Understanding how to adapt your networking approach for different sectors becomes important. Digital platforms enable cross-pollination of ideas and relationships, while traditional networking events provide grounds for unexpected collaborations.

Building Your Industry Presence

Start by identifying key players and platforms in your sector. Develop a reputation for contributing valuable insights to industry discussions. Create content that showcases your expertise while providing genuine value to your professional community. Remember, industry leadership grows from consistent, authentic engagement.

Digital-Traditional Balance

Each industry requires its own balance of digital and traditional networking approaches. Technology professionals might lean heavily toward digital platforms, while healthcare practitioners often benefit more from in-person events. Find the mix that serves your industry and professional goals.

Professional Development Strategy

Create a structured approach to industry engagement. Identify key events, platforms, and communities in your sector. Set specific goals for network development and professional visibility. Regular review and adjustment of your strategy ensures continued relevance and effectiveness.

Future-Focused Networking

Stay attuned to emerging trends in your industry. Build relationships not just for current needs but for future opportunities. Remember that today's junior colleague might be tomorrow's industry leader. Invest in relationships at all levels of your professional ecosystem.

The most successful professionals understand that industry-specific networking isn't about collecting contacts - it's about building a community that supports mutual growth and innovation. Begin by identifying the most relevant networking channels for your industry, then make a sustainable plan for meaningful engagement.

Your professional journey is unique to your industry and goals. Start today by choosing one industry-specific networking initiative and commit to consistent engagement. Remember, meaningful professional relationships develop through sustained, authentic interaction within your industry's unique context.

Your Action Plan for Better Communication:

- Practice presence over perfection
- Try to understand before being understood
- Embrace silence as a tool for deeper connection

- Request feedback regularly
- Choose clarity over complexity

As Anthony Robbins says, "The way we communicate with others and with ourselves ultimately determines the quality of our lives."

Questions to ask yourself and reflect upon:

1. How deeply do you listen in conversations?
2. What barriers prevent deeper connections?
3. How do you build trust in relationships?
4. What makes you memorable to others?
5. How can you improve your connection skills?

CHAPTER TWENTY-SIX: THE PERSONAL JOURNEY OF PROFESSIONAL CONNECTION

THE FOUNDATION of Modern Networking

In today's interconnected world, networking has evolved beyond simple business card exchanges. As Porter Gale wisely noted, "Your network is your net worth," highlighting how genuine professional relationships shape career trajectories. Success comes from understanding that every interaction presents an opportunity for meaningful connection.

Breaking Through Personal Barriers

Jennifer's story resonates with many professionals. As a talented graphic designer, she initially let introversion limit her networking potential. Through deliberate practice and a mindset shift, she transformed her approach to professional connections. Starting with one monthly event, she discovered that authentic networking focused on relationship-building rather than self-promotion.

Cultural Intelligence in Global Networking

Robert's experience in Japan exemplifies modern networking's cultural dimensions. His success came from thorough preparation and genuine respect for cultural differences. By presenting his business card with both hands and adapting his communication style, he built trust that transcended cultural boundaries. This approach shows how cultural sensitivity creates lasting international connections.

The Evolution of Professional Presence

Your professional presence extends across physical and digital realms. Michele Jennae's insight that networking connects "people with people, people with ideas, and people with opportunities" remains relevant across all platforms. Digital presence requires the same authenticity as face-to-face interactions, while offering unique opportunities for ongoing engagement.

Creating Sustainable Value

Ivan Misner's philosophy that "networking is not about using people, it's about helping people" forms the cornerstone of modern professional relationships. Focus on contributing meaningful value to your network through knowledge sharing, introductions, and genuine support. This approach naturally cultivates a community eager to reciprocate.

Strategic Network Development

Begin with clear objectives for your networking efforts. Whether seeking career advancement, client expansion, or industry knowledge, defined goals guide meaningful connections. Regular engagement in professional organizations and industry events provides structured opportunities for network growth.

The Digital-Traditional Balance

Modern networking demands mastery of both digital and traditional channels. LinkedIn serves as your professional home base, while in-person events offer irreplaceable opportunities for deeper connection. Maintain consistent engagement across both spheres to maximize your networking impact.

Building Authentic Professional Relationships

Keith Ferrazzi's observation that "the power of your network is determined by the strength of your relationships" emphasizes quality over quantity. Focus on creating genuine connections through active listening, thoughtful follow-up, and consistent value delivery. These relationships become the foundation of your professional community.

Your Professional Growth Strategy

Develop a structured approach to network building. Start with small, manageable steps like updating your LinkedIn profile or attending one industry event. Gradually expand your efforts as your confidence grows. Track your progress and adjust your strategy based on results and comfort level.

Cultivating Long-term Success

Successful networking requires patience and persistence. Create systems for regular follow-up and relationship maintenance. Remember Jim Rohn's wisdom that "the fortunes of many will be determined by the network they build." Invest time in nurturing professional relationships that support mutual growth.

Looking Forward

The future of professional networking combines traditional relationship-building skills with modern digital tools. Success comes from authenticity, cultural awareness, and consistent value creation. Start your networking journey today by choosing one area for focused improvement. Remember, every strong professional network began with a single connection.

Begin your personal networking transformation by identifying your immediate goals and acting today. Whether digital or traditional, focus on building genuine relationships that create lasting professional value. Your success depends on the connections you begin building now.

Action Items:

Immediate Actions (First 24 Hours)

Define your primary networking objective following Porter Gale's principle. Audit your current professional relationships. Create a basic networking mission statement. Schedule one meaningful connection activity for this week.

First Week Implementation

Update your LinkedIn profile to reflect authentic personal brand. Research one professional organization aligned with your goals. Practice Jennifer's introvert-friendly networking approach. Document your unique value proposition for potential connections.

Cultural Intelligence Development

Study business etiquette for your target markets like Robert did. Create a cultural intelligence cheat sheet for international networking. Practice adapting your communication style for different cultures. Research cross-cultural networking norms.

Digital Presence Enhancement

Establish your professional social media schedule. Create templates for authentic online engagement. Plan your content sharing strategy. Set up a system to track digital networking metrics.

Value Creation Strategy

List three ways you can provide value to your network today. Develop a knowledge-sharing calendar. Identify potential valuable introductions within your network. Create a system for tracking value exchanges.

Monthly Development Goals

Schedule one networking event attendance. Plan three one-on-one connection meetings. Create content for professional platform sharing. Establish regular network maintenance checkpoints.

Relationship Building Framework

Implement Keith Ferrazzi's quality-focused approach: Create a relationship depth assessment tool. Develop follow-up templates for different situations. Schedule regular check-ins with key contacts. Plan relationship nurturing activities.

Professional Growth Metrics

Establish baseline networking measurements. Create progress tracking system. Set specific networking milestones. Plan quarterly networking goal reviews.

Long-term Strategy Development

Design your six-month networking roadmap. Create relationship maintenance schedule. Plan professional development activities. Set long-term connection goals.

Balance Implementation

Create schedule balancing digital and traditional networking. Plan monthly in-person networking activities. Develop online engagement strategy. Set up cross-platform networking system.

Follow-up System Creation

Design personalized follow-up templates. Create follow-up schedule framework. Develop relationship progression markers. Establish regular maintenance checkpoints.

Continuous Improvement Plan

Schedule monthly networking strategy reviews. Create feedback collection system. Plan skill development activities. Set progressive networking challenges.

Remember to start small and build consistently, following Jennifer's example of gradual expansion. Focus on authenticity in every interaction and adjust these action items to match your personal style and professional goals.

Questions to ask yourself and reflect upon:

1. How has your networking style evolved?
2. What relationship patterns do you notice?
3. How do you nurture professional relationships?
4. What networking fears hold you back?
5. How can you make networking more natural?

CHAPTER TWENTY-SEVEN: NETWORKING SUCCESS STORIES AND SOLUTIONS - REAL TRANSFORMATIONS

CAREER TRANSITION TRIUMPHS

Michael's journey from corporate finance to tech entrepreneurship illustrates the power of strategic networking. "I knew making a career pivot would require more than just skills—it would need the right connections," he reflects. Through targeted attendance at tech meetups and consistent engagement in online developer communities, Michael built relationships that eventually led to his first startup's seed funding. His approach focused on learning from others while openly sharing his finance expertise, creating mutual value in every interaction.

The Introvert's Path to Networking Success

Emily, a software architect, transformed her natural introversion into a networking advantage. "Instead of trying to become an extrovert, I leveraged my listening skills," she shares. By focusing on one-on-one conversations and thoughtful follow-ups, Emily built a powerful network that led to speaking opportunities at major tech conferences. Her story shows how authentic networking strategies aligned with personal strengths yield the best results.

International Networking Innovation

When Sarah moved from London to Singapore, she faced the challenge of building a network from scratch in a new cultural context. "Understanding local business etiquette became as important as my professional expertise," she notes. Through a combination of cultural research, local professional associations, and digital networking platforms, Sarah established a thriving cross-cultural network within six months.

Common Challenges and Strategic Solutions

Time Management

James, a busy executive, developed a systematic approach to network maintenance. He dedicates 30 minutes each morning to meaningful connections, using a rotating contact system to ensure regular engagement with key relationships. "Consistency matters more than duration," he emphasizes, highlighting how small, regular efforts maintain strong networks.

Following Up Effectively

Alexandra's success in reactivating dormant networks came from her personalized follow-up strategy. She maintains a digital notebook recording personal details and shared interests from each interaction. "Every follow-up email references something specific from our last conversation," she explains, achieving an 80% response rate through this personal touch.

Measuring Networking Success

Quantitative Metrics

David tracks his networking success through specific metrics: meaningful conversations per month, follow-up meeting conversion rates, and collaborative projects initiated through network connections. "What gets measured gets managed," he notes, attributing his rapid career advancement to this systematic approach.

Qualitative Assessment

Rachel evaluates her network's quality through a relationship depth matrix. She categorizes connections based on interaction frequency, mutual value exchange, and growth potential. "Understanding these patterns helps me invest my networking energy more effectively," she shares.

Network Reactivation Success

Jennifer revived her dormant professional network after a five-year career break through a three-phase approach: digital reconnection, value-first engagement, and in-person meetings. "I focused on offering help before asking for anything," she explains, successfully transitioning back into her industry through these renewed connections.

Strategic Network Development

Digital Platform Optimization

Marcus leveraged LinkedIn's content features to establish thought leadership in his industry. "Regular, insightful posts created organic networking opportunities," he shares. His approach combined industry analysis with personal experience, attracting connections who shared his professional interests.

Cross-Industry Networking

Patricia built a diverse network spanning technology, design, and business sectors. "Cross-pollination of ideas creates unique opportunities," she notes. Her success came from identifying common challenges across industries and helping with solutions through her varied network.

Measuring ROI

Tangible Outcomes

Robert tracks networking ROI through specific metrics: referral business generated, speaking opportunities secured, and collaborative projects initiated. His systematic approach helps justify the time and resources invested in networking activities.

Intangible Benefits

Lisa emphasizes the importance of measuring soft returns: knowledge gained, mentorship opportunities, and personal growth. "Some of the most valuable network benefits can't be quantified traditionally," she observes.

Begin your networking transformation by choosing one success story that resonates with your situation. Adapt their strategies to your context, maintaining authenticity while implementing proven approaches. Remember, every networking success story started with a single connection made with genuine intention.

Action Items:

Immediate Actions (First 24 Hours)

Set aside 30 minutes following James's morning networking ritual. Create a digital notebook for contact management like Alexandra's system. Choose one success story that most closely matches your situation. Draft your first personalized follow-up message using Alexandra's specific-reference approach.

First Week Implementation

Develop your networking metrics dashboard combining David's quantitative and Rachel's qualitative measures. Create a LinkedIn content calendar inspired by Marcus's thought leadership strategy. Schedule three one-on-one conversations, following Emily's introvert-friendly approach. Research and join two relevant professional associations in your industry.

First Month Goals

Establish your personalized follow-up system based on Jennifer's three-phase approach. Create a relationship depth matrix following Rachel's assessment model. Identify cross-industry networking opportunities using Patricia's strategy. Set up a ROI tracking system combining Robert's tangible metrics with Lisa's intangible benefits measurement.

Career Transition Focus

If changing careers, implement Michael's dual approach: go to industry-specific meetups and engage in online communities. Document your current expertise that could provide value in your target industry. Create a networking map of key players in your desired field. Develop your unique value proposition for cross-industry networking.

International/Relocation Networking

For those relocating, follow Sarah's three-pronged approach: Research local business culture and etiquette. Join local professional associations. Establish presence on region-specific digital platforms.

Introvert-Friendly Strategy

Implement Emily's focused approach: Prioritize one-on-one meetings over large events. Prepare thoughtful questions in advance. Schedule regular follow-ups with key contacts. Leverage writing skills through digital platforms.

Network Maintenance System

Create a rotating contact system like James's: Dedicate 30 minutes daily to network maintenance. Establish a regular check-in schedule with key contacts. Develop a content-sharing strategy for staying visible. Set up automatic reminders for follow-ups.

Digital Presence Development

Following Marcus's example: Create a content calendar for LinkedIn posts. Identify your unique industry insights to share. Plan regular engagement with your network's content. Document successful networking outcomes.

Measurement and Tracking

Implement a combined metrics system: Track quantitative measures (David's approach). Document qualitative outcomes (Rachel's method). Monitor ROI using Robert's framework. Record intangible benefits following Lisa's model.

Long-term Strategy Development

Create a six-month networking plan: Set specific growth targets for your network. Plan regular relationship audit intervals. Establish criteria for success in your networking efforts. Schedule quarterly strategy reviews and adjustments.

Remember to adapt these action items to your specific circumstances and industry context. Start with the elements that address your most pressing networking needs, then gradually incorporate additional strategies as you build momentum.

Questions to ask yourself and reflect upon:

1. What networking approaches have worked best for you?
2. How do you learn from others' networking success?
3. What networking strategies could you adapt?
4. How do you measure networking effectiveness?
5. What would make your networking more successful?

CHAPTER TWENTY-EIGHT: ESSENTIAL TOOLS AND TEMPLATES FOR STRATEGIC NETWORKING

DIGITAL RELATIONSHIP MANAGEMENT

Modern networking demands sophisticated tools for maintaining meaningful connections. David, a sales executive, transformed his networking approach using a customized CRM system. "I track every interaction, set follow-up reminders, and note personal details that make future conversations more meaningful," he explains. His system combines Hubspot for professional contacts with a personalized spreadsheet for relationship milestones, creating a comprehensive view of his network's development.

Crafting Authentic Outreach

Sarah's template for LinkedIn connections achieves a remarkable 70% response rate. She personalizes each message by mentioning specific projects and unique insights she's observed in the potential connection's work. Her approach focuses on genuine interest in learning from others, rather than immediate requests for favors or meetings. This authenticity shines through in every message, making her outreach stand out in crowded inboxes.

Follow-up Excellence

Michael developed a sophisticated three-phase follow-up system after networking events. Within 24 hours, he sends a personalized thank you note referencing specific conversation points. A week later, he shares a relevant resource discussed during their interaction. Finally, after a month, he checks in with valuable industry insights. This systematic approach ensures consistent, meaningful follow-up without feeling mechanical or forced.

Reconnection Strategy

Jennifer's approach to rekindling dormant professional relationships focuses on value-first outreach. She begins by sharing relevant articles or insights about their current projects or industry, referencing previous conversations to maintain continuity. This method shows ongoing interest and attention to their professional journey, making reconnection feel natural and welcomed.

Event Preparation Framework

Rachel's conference preparation strategy combines thorough research with strategic planning. She studies speakers and attendees, preparing relevant discussion topics and specific connection goals. Her approach includes creating conversation starters based on the event agenda, ensuring meaningful interactions rather than superficial exchanges.

Virtual Event Excellence

Marcus developed a comprehensive digital networking system that addresses both technical and interpersonal aspects of virtual connections. His approach ensures professional presentation while maintaining authentic engagement. He focuses on creating memorable interactions even through digital platforms, following up with personalized connection requests that reference specific conversation points.

Relationship Nurturing Systems

Alexandra maintains connection strength through carefully timed engagement points throughout the year. She shares industry insights monthly, conducts personal check-ins quarterly, and schedules virtual coffee meetings twice yearly. Her annual network review ensures no valuable connection goes untended, while maintaining authentic relationships rather than mechanical interactions.

Value Addition Framework

Thomas created a system for consistent value delivery within his network. Each week, he identifies three connections who might benefit from specific resources, introductions, or insights. This proactive approach keeps relationships fresh and meaningful while establishing him as a valuable network node.

Implementation Guide

Lisa's framework for industry changes emphasizes relationship building during career transitions. She maps target industry connections, develops relevant skill stories, and creates industry-specific networking scripts. Her approach focuses on building cross-industry value propositions that make connections mutually beneficial.

Geographic Relocation Strategy

Robert's system for building networks in new locations combines digital and physical presence. He immediately joins local professional associations while establishing himself in digital communities. His approach emphasizes quality over quantity, focusing on creating meaningful connections rather than collecting business cards.

Progress Tracking Methods

Emily tracks her networking success through both quantitative and qualitative metrics. She tracks new meaningful connections, follow-up completion rates, and relationship depth indicators. Her system allows for regular assessment of networking effectiveness while maintaining focus on authentic relationship building.

Relationship Quality Assessment

David's quarterly network audit examines the health and potential of his professional relationships. He evaluates interaction frequency, mutual value creation, and strategic alignment. This systematic approach ensures his networking efforts remain focused and effective while maintaining authentic connections.

Begin implementing these tools by selecting one framework that addresses your most pressing networking need. Adapt these templates to your personal style while maintaining authenticity. Remember, these tools enhance, not replace, genuine human connection.

Action Items: Essential Networking Tools Implementation

First 24 Hours

Create a simple relationship tracking document in your preferred format (spreadsheet, CRM, or notebook). Include contact details, last interaction date, and key personal/professional details for your most important connections. Write three personalized follow-up messages to recent contacts using Sarah's value-first template.

First Week

Set up a basic CRM system (like HubSpot free version or Notion) for contact management. Draft your personalized outreach template following Sarah's 70% response rate model. Create a digital calendar for regular check-ins with key contacts. Write one reconnection message to a dormant professional contact using Jennifer's value-first approach.

First Month

Develop your customized event preparation checklist based on Rachel's framework. Create templates for virtual meeting follow-ups. Establish your monthly value-delivery system, identifying three contacts who would benefit from specific resources or introductions. Set up a simple tracking system for networking metrics.

First Quarter

Implement Alexandra's relationship nurturing schedule with customized touchpoints. Conduct your first network audit using David's assessment criteria. Create your personalized follow-up system incorporating Michael's three-phase approach. Establish regular review periods for your networking effectiveness.

Ongoing Development

Schedule monthly reviews of your networking metrics and relationship quality. Create quarterly networking goals aligned with your professional objectives. Maintain your value-first outreach system with regular content sharing and introductions. Adjust your templates based on response rates and feedback.

Professional Growth Integration

Document successful networking interactions and their outcomes. Refine your approach based on what works best for your industry and personality. Develop industry-specific networking scripts for different situations. Create a resource library of valuable content to share with your network.

Network Expansion Strategy

Identify three new professional communities to join. Make a plan for meaningful contribution to these communities. Develop your digital networking presence across relevant platforms. Establish yourself as a valuable resource within your professional ecosystem.

Relationship Quality Focus

Start tracking the depth and quality of your professional relationships. Implement regular value-addition activities for key connections. Create systems for identifying new opportunities to help others. Maintain authenticity in all networking activities.

Remember to adapt these action items to your specific situation and industry context. Start with the most pressing needs and gradually put additional systems into practice as you become comfortable with each new element.

Questions to ask yourself and reflect upon:

1. What networking tools do you currently use?
2. How organized is your contact management?
3. What follow-up systems need improvement?
4. How effectively do you track networking activities?
5. What tools would enhance your networking?

SECTION EIGHT: CHAPTER SUMMARY - NETWORKING/CONNECTING

CHAPTER 24: Networking in the Digital Age

- Evolution of professional networking
- Core networking principles
- Digital networking mastery
- Building authentic connections
- Strategic networking framework
- Implementation strategies
- Advanced networking techniques

Chapter 25: The Art of Connection

- Foundation of active listening

- Nonverbal communication power

- Emotional intelligence factor

- Industry-specific strategies:

  ◦ Technology sector

  ◦ Creative industries

- ○ Business/Financial services

- ○ Healthcare

- ○ Education

- • Digital-Traditional balance

- • Professional development strategy

Chapter 26: The Personal Journey of Professional Connection

- • Modern networking foundation

- • Breaking through personal barriers

- • Cultural intelligence in global networking

- • Professional presence evolution

- • Strategic network development

- • Building authentic relationships

- • Action items for implementation

Chapter 27-28: Success Stories and Essential Tools

- • Career transition examples

- • Introvert's networking path

- • Common challenges and solutions

- • Measuring networking success

- • Digital relationship management

- • Implementation frameworks

- • Progress tracking methods

- • Action items and templates

Key themes across chapters:

- Authenticity in networking

- Balance of digital and traditional approaches

- Strategic relationship building

- Cultural awareness

- Practical implementation tools

SECTION NINE: PERSONAL GROWTH

CHAPTER TWENTY-NINE: THE GROWTH ZONE: WHY EMBRACING DISCOMFORT IS YOUR KEY TO UNLOCKING POTENTIAL

LET'S talk about comfort zones. They're cozy, familiar, and often feel safe. But here's the thing: staying within that comfortable bubble can keep you stuck and prevent you from reaching your full potential. Growth happens outside your comfort zone, and this article will give you tips to help you push past your limitations and embrace a more expansive view of what's possible for you. You're reading this article because you're ready to act, so let's dive in!

The Relationship Between Discomfort and Personal Growth:

Discomfort isn't something to avoid – it's a sign that you're stretching, expanding, and growing. Think about when you learned to ride a bike or started a new job – you probably felt a little (or a lot!) uncomfortable. But through that discomfort, you gained new skills, learned to push your boundaries, and became stronger.

- **Growth Happens Beyond Comfort:** The best changes happen when you move past your perceived limits.
- **Discomfort is a Signal:** It says you are learning, developing, and evolving.

- **Building Resilience:** When you step outside your comfort zone, you build resilience and expand your capacity to handle whatever comes your way.

Tips for Recognizing and Embracing Discomfort:

- **Identify When You're in Your Comfort Zone:** Do you always do the same things and never step outside what's familiar? When you avoid discomfort, you also avoid growth.
- **Acknowledge Discomfort:** Don't run from the feeling of discomfort! Instead, welcome it. It means you're growing! Use your breath to be with that discomfort and then act.
- **Reframe Discomfort:** Instead of viewing discomfort as something negative, see it as a challenge, an invitation for growth, and an opportunity for positive change.
- **Take Small Steps:** You need not make a massive leap all at once. Start with small, manageable actions that move you just slightly outside of your comfort zone and make you feel more able to handle anything that comes your way.
- **Celebrate Progress:** When you step outside your comfort zone, celebrate that effort and that win. It's important to acknowledge and celebrate those moments.
- **Be Kind to Yourself:** Sometimes, discomfort feels overwhelming. Be patient with yourself, celebrate your wins, and keep taking steps forward.

Examples of How Stepping Outside Your Comfort Zone Can Lead to Breakthroughs:

- **Taking on a challenging project at work:** This can lead to new skills, promotions, and new opportunities.
- **Starting a new hobby or creative outlet:** It can bring new joy, new purpose, and new ways of connecting with others.
- **Having a difficult conversation with a loved one:** This can strengthen your relationships and improve communications.

- **Trying something that terrifies you:** This can give you confidence, resilience, and a sense of accomplishment.

Limiting beliefs are those nagging doubts and assumptions that hold you back from meeting your goals and living your best life. They can come from negative self-talk, experiences, or societal messages. But you have the power to change these limiting beliefs and create a life you love!

- **Identifying Limiting Beliefs:** Pay attention to your inner dialogue and identify what it's telling you. Ask yourself: are these thoughts serving me, or are they holding me back?
- **Challenging the Validity of Your Beliefs:** Ask yourself, are these beliefs based on truth, or on assumptions? Where's the evidence that these beliefs are real?
- **Reframing Limiting Beliefs:** Transform those negative thoughts into positive, empowering affirmations and start telling yourself a new story.
- **Action is Key:** The most important thing is to act and move forward, even with discomfort. Discomfort is a signal of growth and change.

Putting it All Together:

By understanding the relationship between discomfort and growth, learning how to embrace that discomfort, and setting goals, you will take command of your life and create an experience that is authentic, purposeful, and fulfilling. Take the first step toward your own growth zone today!

Self-Directed Exercises:

Here are a few exercises to help you embrace discomfort and act:

- **Identify Your Comfort Zone:** What does it look like? What are you avoiding? Journal your answers.
- **Set a Stretch Goal:** Identify a goal that challenges you, and plan to start working toward it today.

- **Embrace Discomfort:** Put yourself in a situation that you find uncomfortable and face it.
- **Celebrate Success:** After acting, reflect on your experience. Celebrate your effort and your success.
- **Surround Yourself with a Community:** Find others who will help you to stay accountable, celebrate your successes, and encourage you to continue reaching for more.

Conclusion:

Embracing discomfort is about pushing your limits and about growing into your best self. It's about choosing to move toward discomfort instead of choosing to avoid it and then using those insights to guide your future choices. The most important thing is to take steps toward that vision today, and to continue growing and evolving. Discomfort isn't your enemy - it's your signal that you are on the right path.

Questions to ask yourself and reflect upon:

1. What keeps you in your comfort zone?

2. When have you grown most through discomfort?

3. What opportunities for growth are you avoiding?

4. How do you support yourself during challenges?

5. What would become possible if you embraced discomfort more?

CHAPTER THIRTY: UNLOCK YOUR POTENTIAL: CULTIVATING A GROWTH MINDSET & BREAKING FREE FROM LIMITING BELIEFS

EVER NOTICE how some people seem to radiate positivity? It's not always a matter of luck or circumstance; it's often about a conscious choice to cultivate a positive attitude. You might be thinking, "Yeah, yeah, easier said than done," and I hear you! But a positive outlook is a skill you *can* learn, and it can transform your life both personally and professionally. Let's explore practical tips that can help you shift your focus and unlock your full potential.

Developing a Positive Attitude in Your Personal Life:

Life isn't always sunshine and rainbows, but how we approach it can make a world of difference. Here are practical tips to cultivate a more positive personal life:

- **Practice Gratitude:** It sounds simple, but it's powerful! Regularly reflect on what you're thankful for. Jot down a few things daily. It helps shift your perspective from what's missing to what's abundant.
- **Surround Yourself with Positivity:** Ever been around someone who just zaps your energy? You know the type – you leave a conversation feeling drained and deflated. Choose to

spend time with people who lift you up, and limit exposure to people who bring you down.

- **Set Reasonable Goals:** We all have dreams, but they can feel overwhelming sometimes. Break them down into smaller, manageable goals. This lets you celebrate achievements and keep moving forward without the feeling of constant stress. Be flexible and realistic with your goal setting.
- **Focus on the Present Moment:** Stop dwelling on the past or worrying about the future! Practice mindfulness and engage in the here and now. This can reduce stress and help you appreciate the present.
- **Engage in Activities You Enjoy:** Carve out time for hobbies and activities that bring you joy. These are not luxuries – they're essential for your wellbeing and can improve your overall outlook.
- **Practice Self-Care:** Taking care of your physical, emotional, and mental health is key. Make sure you're eating well, exercising, getting enough sleep, and seek support from others when you need it. This isn't selfish - it is an act of self-preservation.
- **Be Kind to Yourself:** Cut yourself some slack! Negative self-talk is draining. Replace self-criticism with compassion and positive self-affirmations. You're doing great, even when things aren't perfect.

Developing a Positive Attitude in Your Professional Life:

Your professional life can feel like a roller coaster, but your attitude will keep you in the seat. Here are strategies that will give you greater control over your perspective in the workplace:

- **Practice Gratitude (Again!):** Just as in your personal life, it's important to focus on what you have, rather than what you lack. Be thankful for the opportunities you have, the work you are doing, and the team that you work with.
- **Be Open-Minded:** Seek different viewpoints and be willing to

consider new approaches. Flexibility and adaptability can bring new insights and improve your work quality.

- **Practice Positive Self-Talk:** Replace self-doubt and negativity with positive affirmations. It's amazing what a little self-encouragement can do to keep you on track.
- **Focus on Solutions:** Don't just point out the problems – become a solution-finder! Approach challenges with a positive and proactive attitude to find resolutions.
- **Surround Yourself with Positive People (Again!):** Seek colleagues with positive attitudes and establish relationships with like-minded people. Be the person that lifts others up.
- **Take Care of Yourself (Again!):** Don't ignore the need for rest and good health just because you are at work. Your physical and mental wellbeing matters.
- **Seek Opportunities for Growth:** Push yourself to learn new skills and embrace new challenges. This will help you feel more fulfilled, more confident, and more motivated, even in difficult times.

The Power of Positive Thinking: Inspiring Quotes to Live By

And sometimes, we all need a little extra boost. Here are a few favorite quotes to keep you on track:

- "Positive anything is better than negative nothing." - Elbert Hubbard
- "A positive attitude causes a chain reaction of positive thoughts, events, and outcomes. It is a catalyst, and it sparks extraordinary results." - Wade Boggs
- The power of positive thinking is phenomenal." - Norman Vincent Peale
- "Your positive action combined with positive thinking results in success." - Shiv Khera
- "A positive attitude opens the door to positive opportunities, which leads to a positive life." - Joel Osteen
- "Positive attitudes create a chain reaction of positive thoughts, events and outcomes. Join the chain reaction." - Unknown

- "A positive attitude can really make dreams come true - it did for me." - David Bailey
- "Positive attitudes bring positive results, because attitudes are contagious." - Zig Ziglar
- "Believe in yourself and all that you are. Know that there is something inside you that is greater than any obstacle." - Christian D. Larson
- "Your attitude, not your aptitude, will determine your altitude." - Zig Ziglar.

Conclusion:

A positive attitude isn't about pretending everything's perfect; it's about choosing how you'll respond to life's challenges. By applying these tips, you can transform your mindset, improve your relationships, and meet your goals with greater confidence. So, embrace the power of positivity and start creating a life you love!

Questions to ask yourself and reflect upon:

1. What limiting beliefs hold you back?
2. How do you typically respond to failure?
3. What untapped potential excites you most?
4. How do you cultivate a growth mindset?
5. What support do you need to reach your full potential?

CHAPTER THIRTY-ONE: EMBRACING YOUR AUTHENTIC SELF - THE PATH TO TRUE FULFILLMENT

EMBRACING YOUR AUTHENTIC SELF: **The Path to True Fulfillment**

In our achievement-driven society, many of us find ourselves caught in a relentless pursuit of success, constantly striving to meet societal expectations and live up to unrealistic standards. This unending quest for perfection can leave us feeling overwhelmed, unfulfilled, and disconnected from our true selves. However, there is a path to genuine happiness and contentment – one that begins with embracing our authentic selves, flaws and all.

Key Takeaway:

At the core of our dissatisfaction lies a deep-rooted fear of uncertainty and insecurity. We cling to the illusion of control, believing that if we meet certain goals or reach specific accomplishments, we will finally feel worthy and secure. However, this mindset is ultimately flawed and can lead to a never-ending cycle of dissatisfaction.

True fulfillment comes from learning to accept and love ourselves just as we are, without judgment or conditions. By embracing our flaws, vulnerabilities, and the ever-changing nature of existence, we can find true freedom and contentment.

This concept of self-acceptance is relevant in our fast-paced, achievement-oriented world, where we are constantly bombarded with messages that tell us we are not enough unless we meet certain standards. By internalizing these unrealistic expectations, we perpetuate feelings of inadequacy and self-doubt, which can harm our mental and emotional wellbeing.

Practical Application:

To cultivate self-acceptance, start by practicing mindfulness and self-compassion. Take a few moments each day to check in with yourself, acknowledging your thoughts and emotions without judgment. Treat yourself with the same kindness and understanding you would offer a close friend or loved one.

Another powerful exercise is to list your unique strengths, qualities, and accomplishments, no matter how small they may seem. Celebrate these parts of yourself and remind yourself that your worth is not contingent on external validation or achievements.

Call to Action:

If you're ready to start a transformative journey toward self-acceptance and inner peace, start by making a conscious effort to embrace your authentic self. Surround yourself with supportive individuals who celebrate your unique qualities and encourage your personal growth. Consider seeking guidance from a therapist, counselor, or life coach who can provide valuable insights and techniques to help you along this path.

Action Items:

How to practice good self-care at work or in your career…

· **Take breaks:** Set aside time for short breaks during the day, such as stretching or taking a walk, to refresh your mind and body.

· **Set boundaries:** Establish clear boundaries between work and personal time to reduce stress and prevent burnout.

· **Manage stress:** Practice stress management techniques, such as deep breathing, mindfulness, or physical exercise, to help you stay calm and focused at work.

· Connect with colleagues and participate in team building activities to improve relationships and boost morale in the workplace.

· **Set realistic goals:** Set achievable goals and prioritize your tasks to manage your workload and reduce stress.

· **Speak up:** Communicate your needs and boundaries clearly and assertively and seek support from your colleagues and supervisor when needed.

· **Pursue professional development:** Invest in your career by attending training and workshops, seeking mentorship, or taking courses to improve your skills and knowledge.

· **Celebrate successes:** Take time to acknowledge and appreciate your accomplishments and celebrate the successes of your colleagues.

In a world that often focuses on external validation and societal norms, embracing our authentic selves is a radical act of self-love and liberation. By letting go of the need for constant achievement and control, we can find true freedom and joy in the present moment. This journey toward self-acceptance is not always easy, but the rewards – a deeper sense of inner peace, contentment, and a genuine appreciation for the beauty of life – make it worth the effort.

Here are some motivational quotes about the importance of self-care:

"Self-care is never a selfish act—it is simply good stewardship of the only gift I have, the gift I was put on earth to offer others." - Parker Palmer

"The best investment you can make is in your own abilities. Nobody can take away what you've got in yourself." - Warren Buffett

"Take care of your body. It's the only place you have to live." - Jim Rohn

"It's not selfish to love yourself, take care of yourself, and make your happiness a priority. It's necessary." - Mandy Hale

"The time you enjoy wasting is not wasted time." - Bertrand Russell

"You can't pour from an empty cup. Take care of yourself first." - Unknown

"Self-care is how you take your power back." - Lalah Delia

"Your personal life, your professional life, and your creative life are all intertwined." - Taylor Swift

"You are a unique, valuable and worthy human being, deserving of love and self-care." - Unknown

"To be beautiful means to be yourself. You don't need to be accepted by others. You need to accept yourself." - Thich Nhat Hanh.

Self-care is an essential part of maintaining good physical and mental health. By taking care of yourself, you'll have the energy and motivation to pursue your goals and live a happy and fulfilling life.

I hope these tips will inspire you to make positive changes in your life. Remember that personal and professional growth is a lifelong journey, and every small step counts. Keep learning, keep growing, and keep reaching for your full potential.

Questions to ask yourself and reflect upon:

1. When do you feel most authentically yourself?
2. What masks do you wear in different situations?
3. What parts of yourself do you hide from others?
4. How does authenticity affect your relationships?
5. What would change if you were more authentic?

CHAPTER THIRTY-TWO: THE POWER OF CLARITY - HOW TO DEFINE YOUR VISION AND PRIORITIES FOR EFFECTIVE GOAL SETTING

SUCCESS BEGINS WITH CLARITY. In our fast-paced world, where distractions and opportunities constantly compete for our attention, having a clear vision becomes not just helpful, but essential. Without clarity, we risk spending our precious time and energy pursuing goals that don't truly align with our deepest values and aspirations.

Understanding the Vision-Priority Connection

Vision and priorities are inextricably linked. Your vision represents the destination – the future you want to create. Your priorities are the compass that guides your daily decisions and actions toward that vision. When these two elements align, you create a powerful framework for meaningful goal setting and achievement.

Think of your vision as a detailed photograph of your ideal future. It should encompass all aspects of your life – personal, professional, relationships, health, and legacy. This vision serves as your North Star, helping you navigate decisions and stay focused when challenges arise.

The Journey to Clarity

Gaining clarity requires dedicated time for introspection and honest self-assessment. Start by examining your current situation. What parts of your life bring you joy and fulfillment? Where do you feel frustrated or unfulfilled? These insights provide valuable clues about your true priorities and desires.

Next, project yourself into the future. Imagine yourself five, ten, or twenty years from now. What does your ideal life look like? What achievements make you proud? What relationships have you nurtured? What impact have you made? Be specific and allow yourself to dream big while staying grounded in your values.

Aligning Vision with Values

Your core values serve as the foundation for both your vision and priorities. These fundamental beliefs shape your decisions and determine what matters to you. Identify and articulate your values. They might include things like integrity, creativity, family, personal growth, or community service.

Once you've clarified your values, examine how they align with your current goals and activities. Are you spending time and energy on things that reflect your values? Where do you see misalignment? This analysis often reveals opportunities for meaningful change.

Creating Your Vision Statement

A well-crafted vision statement captures the essence of your desired future in clear, compelling terms. It should be both inspirational and specific enough to guide decision-making. Your vision statement might address:

- Professional accomplishments and impact
- Personal relationships and family life
- Health and wellbeing
- Community involvement and contribution
- Personal growth and learning
- Financial goals and lifestyle

Setting Aligned Priorities

With your vision statement as a guide, you can begin setting priorities that support your larger goals. Consider creating three levels of priorities:

1. Foundation priorities (non-negotiable daily / weekly activities)
2. Growth priorities (activities that move you toward your vision)
3. Enhancement priorities (activities that add value but aren't critical)

Implementation and Action Steps

1. Schedule regular vision review sessions (monthly or quarterly)
2. Create daily routines that support your priorities
3. Develop metrics to track progress toward your vision
4. Build accountability through sharing your vision with trusted allies
5. Regular reassessment and adjustment of priorities as needed

Maintaining Focus and Momentum

Clarity isn't a one-time achievement – it requires ongoing attention and refinement. Schedule regular reviews of your vision and priorities. Are they still aligned with your values? Do they need updating based on new circumstances or insights? This continuous process helps ensure your goals remain relevant and motivating.

Overcoming Obstacles

Expect challenges along the way. External pressures, competing demands, and self-doubt can all threaten to blur your clear vision. Develop strategies to maintain clarity during difficult times:

- Return to your written vision statement
- Reconnect with your core values
- Seek support from mentors or coaches
- Adjust tactics while maintaining strategic direction

. . .

Conclusion:

Clarity is the foundation of effective goal setting and achievement. By investing time in defining your vision and aligning your priorities, you make a powerful framework for decision-making and action. Start today by setting aside quiet time for reflection and vision-crafting. Remember, clarity isn't about perfection – it's about progress toward a meaningful and fulfilling future.

Your future success begins with the clarity you create today. Step toward defining your vision and watch as your goals become not just achievable, but inevitable. The journey to your ideal future starts with a clear understanding of where you want to go and what matters to you.

Questions to ask yourself and reflect upon:

1. How clear are you about your life's direction?
2. What areas of your life need more clarity?
3. How do you gain clarity when feeling confused?
4. What blocks you from seeing clearly?
5. How could increased clarity transform your decisions?

CHAPTER THIRTY-THREE: UNLOCKING THE POWER OF A POSITIVE MINDSET - A LIFE-CHANGING JOURNEY

In today's fast-paced and often stressful world, maintaining a positive attitude can seem like a daunting task. However, cultivating a positive mindset is beneficial for our mental wellbeing and has the power to transform our lives in profound ways. Join us on an inspiring journey as we explore the secrets to developing a positive attitude and unlocking a world of possibilities.

Common Challenge: Overcoming Negative Self-Talk

One of the most significant challenges we face in developing a positive attitude is the constant barrage of negative self-talk that can cloud our minds. We are our own harshest critics, often dwelling on past failures, doubting our abilities, and letting fear hold us back. However, by recognizing and challenging these negative thought patterns, we can reclaim control and cultivate a more optimistic outlook.

Key Takeaway: Gratitude as a Catalyst for Positivity

One of the most powerful tools in fostering a positive attitude is the practice of gratitude. When we shift our focus from what we lack to appreciating the blessings we have, our perspective begins to change. Gratitude opens our hearts and minds, showing the beauty in even the most challenging circumstances. By cultivating an attitude of gratitude, we invite more positivity into our lives and create a ripple effect that extends far beyond ourselves.

Practical Application: The Gratitude Journal

A simple yet effective way to incorporate gratitude into your daily routine is by keeping a gratitude journal. Each day, take a few moments to reflect on the things you are grateful for, no matter how small they may seem. This practice trains your mind to seek the positive aspects of your life, gradually shifting your perspective toward a more optimistic outlook.

Action Steps to Develop a Positive Attitude in Your Career:

1. **Practice mindfulness:** Take a few minutes each day to focus on the present moment and let go of negative thoughts or worries. This can help you maintain a positive outlook and reduce stress.
2. **Seek new experiences:** Try new things, both in and outside of work, to broaden your horizons and build confidence. This can help you maintain a positive attitude, even in difficult situations.
3. **Surround yourself with positive people:** Seek coworkers, friends, and mentors who have a positive outlook and are supportive of your goals and aspirations.
4. **Focus on the good:** Make a habit of noticing and focusing on the positive aspects of your job, your colleagues, and your life. This can help you maintain a positive outlook, even in challenging situations.
5. **Set achievable goals:** Establish clear, achievable goals for your career and track your progress toward them. This will help you feel more in control of your career and increase your sense of accomplishment.
6. **Practice gratitude:** Make a daily habit of listing the things you're grateful for, including your job and the people in your life. This can help you maintain a positive outlook and boost your happiness.

7. **Learn from mistakes:** Instead of dwelling on mistakes, focus on learning from them. This can help you maintain a positive attitude and build resilience, even in the face of failure.

Call to Action: Embrace the Power of Positivity

A positive attitude is a journey, and like any journey, it requires commitment, patience, and perseverance. But the rewards are immeasurable. By embracing the power of positivity, you open yourself up to new opportunities, deeper connections, and a greater sense of fulfillment. Take the first step today and witness the transformative impact a positive mindset can have on your life.

Conclusion: A Brighter Path Ahead

The path to a positive attitude is not always easy, but with the right tools and mindset, it is attainable for all of us. A positive attitude is not about ignoring life's challenges but about approaching them with resilience, hope, and a willingness to grow. By cultivating gratitude, challenging negative thought patterns, and surrounding ourselves with positivity, we can start a journey of personal growth and unlock a world of possibilities. Embrace the power of a positive mindset, and let it be your guiding light toward a brighter, more fulfilling future.

Here are some motivational quotes to help you develop a positive attitude:

1. "Positive anything is better than negative nothing." - Elbert Hubbard
2. "A positive attitude causes a chain reaction of positive thoughts, events, and outcomes. It is a catalyst, and it sparks extraordinary results." - Wade Boggs
3. "Keep a positive mind and a grateful heart." - Unknown
4. "An attitude of positive expectation is the mark of the superior personality." - Brian Tracy
5. "Choose to be optimistic, it feels better." - Dalai Lama

6. "The more you praise and celebrate your life, the more there is in life to celebrate." - Oprah Winfrey
7. "A positive attitude can change everything." - Unknown
8. "Happiness is not something readymade. It comes from your own actions." - Dalai Lama
9. "The only way to do great work is to love what you do." - Steve Jobs
10. "Gratitude turns what we have into enough." - Unknown

A positive attitude can change the way you experience life. By focusing on the good and being grateful, you can attract more positivity into your life.

I hope these tips will inspire you to make positive changes in your life. Remember that personal and professional growth is a lifelong journey, and every small step counts. Keep learning, keep growing, and keep reaching for your full potential.

Questions to ask yourself and reflect upon:

1. What negative thought patterns do you notice?
2. How does your mindset affect your outcomes?
3. What helps you maintain positivity during challenges?
4. How do you reset when negativity creeps in?
5. What would change with a more positive mindset?

CHAPTER THIRTY-FOUR: THE POWER OF POSITIVE SELF-TALK - UPLIFT YOURSELF TO ACHIEVE GREATNESS

BATTLING SELF-DOUBT: A Common Challenge

We've all been there – facing a daunting task or a new challenge, and that little voice in our head starts whispering doubts. "You're not good enough," it says. "You're going to fail." These negative thoughts can be crippling, holding us back from reaching our full potential.

But what if we could silence that inner critic and replace it with a cheerleader? That's the power of positive self-talk.

The Psychological Origins of Self-Talk

Our internal dialogue, or self-talk, is deeply rooted in our past experiences, beliefs, and conditioning. Negative self-talk often stems from childhood experiences, such as criticism from parents or teachers, or from societal pressures to conform to certain standards.

These early experiences can create deeply ingrained beliefs about ourselves, such as "I'm not smart enough" or "I'm not worthy of success." These beliefs then manifest as negative self-talk, reinforcing the cycle of self-doubt and limiting our potential.

Personal Anecdote: Susan's Self-Talk Transformation

Susan, a talented graphic designer, had always dreamed of starting her own business. However, every time she thought about taking the leap, her inner critic would pipe up: "You're not experienced enough. You'll never be able to compete with the big agencies."

These negative thoughts kept Susan stuck in her day job, afraid to pursue her true passion. One day, a friend recommended she try positive self-talk. Skeptical but desperate for a change, Susan gave it a try.

She started by noticing her negative self-talk patterns. Every time she caught herself thinking, "I can't do this," she would reframe it as, "I'm capable of learning and growing." When her inner critic said, "You're not good enough," she would respond with, "I have unique skills and perspectives to offer."

At first, it felt unnatural and forced. But as Susan continued to practice, something remarkable happened. Her confidence grew, and she took small steps toward her dream. She enrolled in a business course, contacted potential clients, and started building her portfolio.

As Susan's self-talk became more positive, her actions followed. Within a year, she had quit her day job and launched her own successful design agency. By changing her internal dialogue, Susan had transformed her life.

Exercises to Transform Your Self-Talk

1. **Awareness is key:** Start by simply noticing your self-talk. When do negative thoughts arise? What triggers them? Write down your observations in a journal.
2. **Challenge negative beliefs:** When you catch yourself engaging in negative self-talk, ask yourself, "Is this really true?" Look for evidence to the contrary. For example, if you think, "I'm not good at public speaking," remind yourself of times when you've spoken up in meetings or given presentations.

3. **Create positive affirmations:** Craft positive statements that counter your negative beliefs. For example, instead of "I'm not smart enough," try "I am capable of learning and growing." Repeat these affirmations daily, especially when negative thoughts arise.

4. **Practice self-compassion:** Treat yourself with kindness and understanding, as you would a good friend. When you make a mistake or face a setback, instead of berating yourself, try saying something like, "Everyone makes mistakes. What can I learn from this?"

5. **Visualize success:** Imagine yourself succeeding in your goals. What does it look and feel like? How are you talking to yourself in these moments? Regularly visualizing positive outcomes can help rewire your self-talk patterns.

Remember, transforming your self-talk is a process. Be patient with yourself and celebrate each small victory along the way.

Key Takeaway: Positive Self-Talk as Your Personal Cheerleader

Positive self-talk is the practice of intentionally reframing negative thoughts into positive, encouraging statements. It's like having a supportive friend inside your head, reminding you of your strengths and capabilities.

Imagine facing that big presentation or job interview. Instead of dwelling on doubts, you tell yourself, "I've prepared thoroughly, and I'm capable of nailing this." This simple shift in mindset can make all the difference in boosting your confidence and performance.

Practical Application: Start Small and Build Momentum

Incorporating positive self-talk into your daily life can be transformative, but it takes practice. Start by learning of your negative thought patterns and consciously replacing them with positive affirmations.

For example, instead of saying "I'm terrible at public speaking," try "I'm working on improving my public speaking skills, and I'm getting better every time."

It may feel awkward at first but stick with it. The more you practice positive self-talk, the more natural and empowering it will become.

Action Steps:

Use Positive Self-Talk in Your Career.

1. **Identify negative self-talk patterns:** Start by becoming aware of your negative thoughts about yourself in the workplace. Write them down and try to understand where they come from.
2. **Reframe negative thoughts:** Once you have identified negative self-talk patterns, challenge them by reframing them into positive ones. For example, instead of saying "I'm not good enough for this job," try saying "I have the skills and experience necessary to succeed in this role."
3. **Practice gratitude:** Make a daily habit of listing the things you're grateful for, including your strengths and accomplishments. This will help shift your focus away from negative self-talk.
4. **Surround yourself with positive people:** Seek supportive coworkers and mentors who can provide encouragement and motivation.
5. **Set achievable goals:** Break down large tasks into smaller, achievable goals, and celebrate your progress along the way. This will give you a sense of accomplishment and boost your confidence.
6. **Focus on solutions:** Instead of dwelling on problems, focus on finding solutions. This will help you maintain a positive outlook, even in challenging situations.
7. **Visualize success:** Imagine yourself succeeding in your career, and see yourself as confident, capable, and successful. This will help you cultivate a positive self-image.

Call to Action: Embrace the Power Within

Positive self-talk is a powerful tool, but it's the beginning. By believing in yourself and speaking kindly to yourself, you'll gain the confidence and resilience to tackle any challenge life throws your way.

So, why not start today? Silence that inner critic and let your personal cheerleader take the lead. You've got this!

Conclusion: A Journey of Self-Discovery and Growth

Positive self-talk is a profound practice that can transform your life, but it's not a quick fix. It's a journey of self-discovery, self-acceptance, and personal growth.

As you continue to nurture a positive inner dialogue, you'll become more resilient, more confident, and more capable of achieving your dreams.

You are your own greatest ally. Treat yourself with kindness, compassion, and encouragement, and watch as doors open and obstacles crumble before you.

The path to greatness starts with believing in yourself. Embrace the power of positive self-talk, and let it guide you on your journey to becoming the best version of yourself.

Here are motivational quotes about the power of positive self-talk:

1. "Your thoughts become your words. Your words become your actions. Your actions become your habits. Your habits become your values. Your values become your destiny." - Mahatma Gandhi
2. "The way we talk to ourselves matters more than anything anyone else can say." - Unknown
3. "Your mind is a powerful thing. When you fill it with positive thoughts, your life will start to change." – Unknown
4. "Words have power. Speak to yourself like you would to someone you love." - Brené Brown

I hope these tips will inspire you to make positive changes in your life. Remember that personal and professional growth is a lifelong journey, and every small step counts. Keep learning, keep growing, and keep reaching for your full potential.

Questions to ask yourself and reflect upon:

1. What messages do you tell yourself most often?
2. How does your self-talk affect your confidence?
3. What negative self-talk patterns need changing?
4. How do you encourage yourself during difficulties?
5. What positive messages need more reinforcement?

CHAPTER THIRTY-FIVE: THE MIND-BODY CONNECTION - UNDERSTANDING HOW THOUGHTS SHAPE YOUR HEALTH AND WELLBEING

OUR MENTAL AND physical health are intricately interconnected, forming a powerful relationship that influences every aspect of our wellbeing. Understanding and harnessing this connection can transform our health, happiness, and overall quality of life.

The Science Behind the Mind-Body Connection

Modern research continues to unveil the fascinating ways our thoughts influence our physical health. When we experience negative thoughts or stress, our bodies release cortisol and other stress hormones, triggering our "fight-or-flight" response. Chronic activation of this stress response can lead to various health issues, including:

- Weakened immune function
- Digestive disorders
- Cardiovascular problems
- Sleep disturbances
- Chronic inflammation
- Accelerated aging
- Mental health challenges

But positive thoughts and emotions stimulate the production of beneficial hormones and neurotransmitters, including serotonin, dopamine, and endorphins. These chemicals promote healing, boost immunity, enhance cognitive function, and improve overall physical health.

The Power of Positive Thinking

Cultivating a positive mindset isn't about denying life's challenges or maintaining unrealistic optimism. Instead, it involves developing a balanced, resilient perspective that acknowledges difficulties while maintaining hope and confidence in our ability to overcome them.

Research demonstrates that positive thinking can:

- Lower blood pressure
- Reduce inflammation
- Strengthen immune response
- Improve cardiovascular health
- Enhance mental clarity
- Promote better sleep
- Accelerate physical healing

Practical Strategies for Strengthening the Mind-Body Connection

1. Mindfulness Practice

Develop awareness of your thoughts through regular mindfulness meditation. This practice helps you observe your mental patterns without judgment and creates space between thoughts and reactions.

2. Thought Monitoring

Keep a thought journal to track recurring mental patterns. Notice how different thoughts affect your physical sensations, energy levels, and overall wellbeing.

3. Cognitive Restructuring

Learn to challenge and reframe negative thought patterns. Replace self-defeating thoughts with balanced, constructive alternatives that promote health and resilience.

4. Body Awareness

Practice regular body scans to notice physical tensions and release them through conscious relaxation. This strengthens your ability to recognize and address stress responses early.

5. Healthy Lifestyle Integration

Combine positive thinking with healthy lifestyle choices:

- Regular physical exercise
- Balanced nutrition
- Adequate sleep
- Stress management techniques
- Social connection

Creating Lasting Change

Transforming your thought patterns requires patience and consistent practice. Start with small, manageable steps:

1. Begin each day with positive intentions
2. Practice gratitude regularly
3. Surround yourself with supportive people
4. Celebrate small victories
5. Learn from challenges rather than dwelling on them

The Role of Professional Support

Consider working with qualified professionals who can guide your journey:

- Mental health counselors
- Health coaches
- Mindfulness instructors
- Holistic health practitioners
- Medical professionals who understand the mind-body connection

Daily Practices for Enhanced Wellbeing

Incorporate these activities into your daily routine:

1. Morning meditation or reflection
2. Physical movement or exercise
3. Mindful breathing exercises
4. Positive affirmations
5. Evening gratitude practice

Conclusion: Your Path to Holistic Health

Understanding and harnessing the mind-body connection opens new possibilities for improving your health and wellbeing. By cultivating awareness of your thoughts and intentionally choosing positive mental patterns, you can create profound changes in both your physical and mental health.

This journey is personal and ongoing. Start where you are, make small consistent changes, and celebrate your progress along the way. As you develop a more positive mindset, you'll likely notice improvements in your energy, resilience, and overall health.

Take the first step today by choosing one simple practice to implement. Whether it's a five-minute meditation, a gratitude journal, or a daily walk with positive affirmations, each small action contributes to your transformation. Your mind and body are powerful allies in creating the vibrant, healthy life you deserve.

Questions to ask yourself and reflect upon:

1. How does your mental state affect your physical health?
2. What stress signals does your body send?
3. How do you maintain mind-body balance?
4. What practices strengthen your mind-body connection?
5. How can you better listen to your body's wisdom?

CHAPTER THIRTY-SIX:
UNLOCK YOUR POTENTIAL -
THE POWER OF A POSITIVE
ATTITUDE IN LIFE
AND WORK
INTRODUCTION:

HAVE you ever felt like you were held back by invisible barriers? Like something inside you says, "you can't," "you're not good enough," or "it's too late for you?" That's the power of limiting beliefs and a fixed mindset at work. But what if I told you you could learn to break free from these self-imposed chains and unlock your true potential? It's possible with a powerful shift in perspective and learning to cultivate a growth mindset, and this article will give you the tips you need to make that shift. So, let's dive in, and start your journey toward becoming your best self!

What is a Growth Mindset?

A growth mindset is the empowering belief that your abilities, intelligence, and talents can be developed through dedication and hard work. It's the opposite of a "fixed mindset," which is the limiting belief that your abilities are set in stone. If you have a growth mindset, you see challenges as opportunities to learn, failures as feedback, and your potential as limitless.

- **Growth Mindset:** You believe that your potential is malleable and can be stretched through effort and learning. You see challenges as opportunities, view criticism as valuable feedback, and see setbacks as a source of knowledge.

- **Fixed Mindset:** You believe your abilities are fixed and can't be changed. You might shy away from challenges, take feedback personally, and give up at the first sign of difficulty.

Why Cultivate a Growth Mindset?

A growth mindset can profoundly impact all areas of your life:

- **Career:** With a growth mindset, you're more likely to embrace new challenges, learn new skills, and take risks that can lead to career advancement and new opportunities.
- **Relationships:** You see disagreements as opportunities for learning and growth, rather than threats to your ego. You're more willing to listen to others, understand their perspectives, and grow closer to those around you.
- **Personal Development**: You embrace learning and continuous growth, viewing setbacks as temporary and surmountable, and seeing the process as more valuable than reaching a specific milestone.

Practical Strategies for Developing a Growth Mindset:

- **Reframe Your Self-Talk:** Turn negative, limiting thoughts into positive, growth-oriented statements. Instead of "I can't do this," try, "I can learn how to do this."
- **Embrace Challenges:** Look for opportunities to step outside your comfort zone, and welcome new experiences that stretch your abilities.
- **Learn from Setbacks:** When you encounter a setback, don't see it as a failure, but as an opportunity to learn valuable lessons and improve your approach. Take the lessons, and then keep going!
- **Surround Yourself with Growth-Minded People:** Seek individuals who inspire you and support your journey to

achieve your best self and look to them as examples of what's possible.

Limiting beliefs are those pesky thoughts and assumptions that hold you back from meeting your goals and living your best life. These beliefs, often rooted in past hurts, societal conditioning, or negative self-talk, can make you feel like you're not good enough, smart enough, or worthy enough to pursue your dreams. But here's the good news: you have the power to break free from these chains and create a life that you love!

Recognizing and Challenging Limiting Beliefs:

- **Become Aware:** Pay attention to your inner dialogue and notice the negative thoughts that often surface. Journal about your fears, insecurities, and self-doubts to shed light on your limiting beliefs.
- **Challenge the Validity:** Ask yourself if these beliefs are based on facts or just assumptions based on your experiences.
- **Reframe the Belief:** Turn the negative belief into an empowering statement that affirms your potential and promotes a more positive mindset.

Techniques for Overcoming Limiting Beliefs:

- **Cognitive Reframing:** Challenge negative thoughts and look at situations from different perspectives. Replace disempowering thoughts with more constructive ones.
- **Affirmations:** Create powerful, positive statements that reflect your worth and potential.
- **Seeking Evidence:** Actively look for proof that disproves the limiting beliefs and promotes confidence.

Putting it All Together:

Let's be clear - overcoming limiting beliefs and developing a growth mindset isn't a one-time event - it's a journey! But by understanding these principles, setting realistic goals, embracing discomfort, and building a supportive community, you'll be on your way toward creating a more fulfilling life and reaching your goals. You need not do it all at once, just start with the first step.

Self-Directed Exercises:

Now it's time to put this into practice! Here are a few exercises to help your mindset shift:

- **Identifying Limiting Beliefs:**
  - Journal about the negative thoughts and limiting beliefs that often surface in your mind.
  - Consider the areas in your life that feel "stuck." What beliefs are keeping you in place?
  - Ask yourself: What do I believe about my abilities, worth, or potential?
- **Challenging and Reframing Beliefs:**
  - Choose a limiting belief you want to work on and write it out.
  - Question its validity. Is this belief based on fact or assumptions?
  - Reframe the belief into a positive and empowering statement.
  - Create 3-5 specific affirmations that challenge this belief and use them daily to help change your perspective.
- **Cultivating a Growth Mindset:**
  - Reflect on a recent challenge or setback. How can you use a growth mindset to interpret this experience?
  - Identify the lessons you've learned and how those will help you.
  - Write statements that will help you to reframe your self-talk in challenging moments.
- **Embracing Discomfort and Taking Action:**
  - Identify a goal that you want to work toward, even if it feels difficult or outside of your comfort zone.
  - Break the goal down into smaller, actionable steps.

- Each day, take action toward your goal and reflect on your experience.
- **Building a Supportive Network:**
  - List the people in your life who embody a growth mindset and make you feel inspired.
  - Identify an area where you would benefit from more support or mentorship and seek people to help you.
  - Connect with a community of others on a similar path.

Conclusion:

Developing a growth mindset and breaking free from limiting beliefs will not only change your future, it will transform your experience in the day to day. Embrace challenges, view failures as valuable lessons, and believe in your endless potential, and you will achieve new heights and be the best version of yourself. Start this process now and let your true potential shine!

Questions to ask yourself and reflect upon:

1. What holds you back from reaching your potential?
2. How do you challenge yourself to grow?
3. What support systems aid your development?
4. How do you measure personal growth?
5. What new possibilities excite you most?

~

CHAPTER THIRTY-SEVEN: UNLOCK THE TRANSFORMATIVE POWER OF COGNITIVE RESTRUCTURING

UNDERSTANDING COGNITIVE RESTRUCTURING

Our thoughts shape our reality. The way we interpret events, experiences, and ourselves creates the framework through which we view the world. When negative thought patterns dominate our mental landscape, they can create barriers to our happiness, success, and personal growth. Cognitive restructuring offers a powerful solution to break free from these mental constraints and create lasting positive change.

The Science of Thought Patterns

Research in cognitive psychology demonstrates that our thoughts directly influence our emotions, behaviors, and overall wellbeing. Common cognitive distortions can significantly impair our mental health. These include patterns like all-or-nothing thinking, where we view situations in absolute terms without acknowledging nuance. Overgeneralization leads us to draw broad conclusions from single events. Catastrophizing causes us to assume the worst possible outcomes, while personalization makes us take excessive responsibility for events beyond our control. Mental filtering, emotional reasoning, should statements, and labeling further compound these distortions, creating a web of negative thinking that can be challenging to escape.

Breaking the Cycle of Negative Thinking

Cognitive restructuring provides a systematic approach to identifying, challenging, and transforming unhelpful thought patterns. This process begins with developing awareness of our thoughts as they occur. We then analyze these thoughts critically, examining the evidence that supports or contradicts them. From there, we generate more balanced perspectives and practice implementing these new thought patterns in our daily lives.

Practical Implementation Strategies

The Thought Record Method serves as a powerful tool for transformation. By maintaining a detailed log of thoughts, emotions, and situations, we can better understand our mental patterns. This record should include the triggering situation, automatic thoughts that arise, emotional and physical responses, and a thorough analysis of the evidence. Through this process, we develop alternative perspectives and evaluate outcomes.

The ABCD Technique provides another structured approach to cognitive restructuring. This method examines the Activating Event, explores our Beliefs and thoughts, considers the Consequences (both emotional and behavioral), and helps us Dispute and develop alternatives to our initial reactions.

Advanced Cognitive Restructuring Techniques

Reframing perspectives becomes crucial in cognitive restructuring. We learn to view situations through different lenses, considering growth opportunities, learning experiences, character-building moments, and potential future benefits. This broader context helps break the cycle of negative interpretation.

Emotional intelligence development goes hand in hand with cognitive restructuring. By recognizing emotional triggers and understanding the connection between thoughts and emotions, we develop stronger emotional regulation skills and build lasting resilience.

Implementation in Daily Life

Creating a supportive daily routine enhances the effectiveness of cognitive restructuring. Begin each morning by setting positive intentions and reviewing empowering beliefs. Throughout the day, pause regularly to check your thoughts and apply restructuring techniques. End each day with reflection, acknowledging progress and planning for continued improvement.

Creating Lasting Change

Building supporting habits requires consistent practice. Regular mindfulness, journaling, positive affirmations, and visualization exercises help reinforce new thought patterns. Working with accountability partners can provide additional support and motivation.

Progress measurement becomes essential for maintaining momentum. Track mood changes, track behavior shifts, and document success stories while remaining mindful of areas for growth.

Advanced Applications

Cognitive restructuring extends beyond personal development into professional growth. The techniques enhance leadership capabilities, decision-making processes, problem-solving abilities, and communication skills. In personal life, these skills improve relationships, goal achievement, stress management, and self-confidence.

Conclusion: Your Journey to Mental Freedom

Cognitive restructuring offers a transformative pathway to reshaping your mindset and creating lasting positive change. Through consistent practice, you can break free from limiting beliefs, enhance emotional wellbeing, and strengthen your decision-making abilities. This journey leads to improved relationships and greater resilience in facing life's challenges.

Begin your transformation today by selecting one technique to implement. Start small, maintain consistency, and celebrate your progress along the way. Transformation unfolds gradually through dedicated practice. Your thoughts create your reality, and by mastering cognitive restructuring, you take control of your mental landscape and, consequently, your life's direction.

The perfect moment to begin this journey is now. As you put these strategies into practice, watch positive changes unfold across every part of your life. Your future self will thank you for taking this important step toward mental freedom and personal empowerment.

Questions to ask yourself and reflect upon:

1. What thought patterns limit your success?
2. How do you challenge unhelpful thoughts?
3. What new perspectives could serve you better?
4. How do you maintain positive thought patterns?
5. What beliefs need restructuring?

CHAPTER THIRTY-EIGHT: THE POWER OF SELF-AWARENESS IN OVERCOMING LIMITING BELIEFS

EVERY JOURNEY of personal transformation begins with a single, powerful step: becoming aware of the invisible barriers that hold us back. These barriers, our limiting beliefs, shape our decisions, actions, and ultimately, our reality. Yet they are not immutable truths but rather stories we've internalized through experience and conditioning.

Understanding Limiting Beliefs

Limiting beliefs run like silent architects of our lives, constructing boundaries we never consciously chose. They manifest in thoughts like "I'm not talented enough, "Success isn't meant for people like me," or "I don't deserve happiness." These beliefs feel true because we've carried them for so long, but they're merely interpretations of experiences, not facts about our potential.

The Journey to Self-Awareness

Self-awareness emerges through conscious observation of our thoughts, emotions, and behavioral patterns. This awareness becomes the flashlight that illuminates the dark corners of our minds where limiting beliefs hide. Through self-awareness, we begin to recognize the gap between who we are and who we believe ourselves to be.

Developing Your Self-Awareness Practice

The path to self-awareness requires dedication and consistent practice. Start by creating quiet moments for self-reflection each day. During these moments, observe your thoughts without judgment, as if watching clouds pass across the sky. Notice the recurring patterns, the self-critical voice, and the assumptions that color your worldview.

Journaling becomes a powerful ally in this process. Through writing, we externalize our internal dialogue, making it easier to examine our beliefs objectively. Write about your fears, dreams, and the stories you tell yourself about what's possible. Look for patterns in your narrative and question their origins.

Understanding Your Emotional Landscape

Our emotions often serve as signposts pointing toward limiting beliefs. When you feel triggered, frustrated, or stuck, pause to explore the beliefs underlying these emotional responses. Ask yourself: What story am I telling myself in this moment? What assumption am I making about my capabilities or worth?

The Role of Past Experiences

Many limiting beliefs take root in experiences, particularly during childhood and early adulthood. Understanding this historical context helps us approach our beliefs with compassion while recognizing their impermanence. Your experiences shaped these beliefs, but they need not determine your future.

Creating New Neural Pathways

As you identify limiting beliefs, you can begin the work of creating new, empowering narratives. This process involves more than positive thinking—it requires consistent practice in redirecting your thoughts and taking actions that challenge your old beliefs. Each small success builds evidence for your new, empowering story.

The Power of Environmental Design

Your environment significantly influences your beliefs and self-awareness. Surround yourself with people who reflect your potential rather than your limitations. Create spaces that inspire growth and possibility. Choose media and activities that reinforce your desired beliefs rather than your fears.

Taking Inspired Action

Self-awareness without action remains purely theoretical. As you uncover limiting beliefs, take small, consistent steps that challenge these beliefs. Start with actions that feel slightly uncomfortable but achievable. Each success builds confidence and erodes the power of limiting beliefs.

Navigating Setbacks

The journey of overcoming limiting beliefs isn't linear. Expect moments of doubt and regression. These aren't failures but opportunities to deepen your self-awareness and strengthen your commitment to growth. Use setbacks as data points rather than confirmation of limiting beliefs.

Cultivating Self-Compassion

Self-awareness must be paired with self-compassion. As you uncover limiting beliefs, approach yourself with kindness and understanding. Remember these beliefs developed as protective mechanisms, even if they no longer serve you.

Creating Lasting Change

Sustainable transformation requires integration of new beliefs at both conscious and unconscious levels. This happens through consistent practice, supportive relationships, and regular reflection on your progress. Celebrate small wins and acknowledge how far you've come.

Conclusion: Your Journey Forward

The path to overcoming limiting beliefs through self-awareness is both challenging and profoundly rewarding. As you develop greater awareness of your thoughts, emotions, and patterns, you gain the power to choose new beliefs that align with your highest potential.

Remember this journey is uniquely yours. Move at your own pace, trust your intuition, and remain committed to your growth. Each moment of awareness creates an opportunity for choice, and each choice shapes your future self.

Start today by taking one small step toward greater self-awareness. Whether through journaling, meditation, or honest self-reflection, begin the process of illuminating your limiting beliefs. Your future self will thank you for having the courage to look within and choose a new path forward.

Questions to ask yourself and reflect upon:

1. How well do you understand your triggers?
2. What patterns do you notice in your behavior?
3. How do your emotions influence your actions?
4. What blind spots might you have?
5. How can you deepen your self-awareness?

CHAPTER THIRTY-NINE: REWRITING YOUR MENTAL SCRIPTS - COGNITIVE REFRAMING TECHNIQUES FOR SUCCESS

THE VOICE in our head shapes our reality more powerfully than any external force. When that voice speaks in limiting beliefs and negative self-talk, it creates invisible barriers to our success and fulfillment. Cognitive reframing offers a transformative path to reshaping these mental narratives and unlocking our true potential.

Understanding Cognitive Reframing

Cognitive reframing is more than positive thinking—it's a systematic approach to identifying, challenging, and transforming limiting thought patterns. This powerful technique lets us consciously shift our perspective, replacing self-defeating narratives with empowering alternatives. Through consistent practice, we can rewire our neural pathways and create lasting positive change.

The Science Behind Mental Scripts

Our brains naturally create mental shortcuts and patterns based on experiences. These patterns, or scripts, influence how we interpret events and make decisions. While this mechanism evolved to help us navigate life efficiently, it can also perpetuate limiting beliefs and negative thought patterns. Understanding this neurological basis helps us approach reframing with patience and scientific clarity.

Transforming Limiting Beliefs

Mental scripts often manifest as seemingly unshakable truths: "I'm not creative enough," "Success isn't for people like me," or "I always fail at important things." However, these beliefs are interpretations, not facts. Through cognitive reframing, we can challenge these assumptions and create new, empowering narratives that better serve our growth and success.

Advanced Reframing Techniques

The Evidence Method

When facing a limiting belief, gather evidence that contradicts it. Create a detailed list of past successes, positive feedback, and moments of growth. This concrete evidence helps challenge the validity of negative self-talk.

Perspective Shifting

Imagine viewing your situation through the eyes of someone you admire. How would they interpret this challenge? What advice would they offer? This shift in perspective often reveals new possibilities and solutions.

Future Self Visualization

Envision your future self who has overcome current limitations. What wisdom would they share? How did they navigate present challenges? This technique helps bridge the gap between current limiting beliefs and future potential.

The Language of Empowerment

Words carry immense power in shaping our reality. Transform limiting language into empowering alternatives:

- "I can't" becomes "I'm learning to"
- "I should" becomes "I choose to"

- "I'm not good enough" "becomes "I'm growing and improving every day"
- "This is impossible" becomes "This is challenging, and I'm finding ways to succeed"

Creating New Neural Pathways

Lasting change requires consistent practice. Each time you catch and reframe a limiting thought, you strengthen new neural pathways. Over time, empowering thoughts become your default response to challenges.

Practical Implementation Strategies

Morning Mental Programming

Start each day by consciously setting your mental tone. Write down potential challenges and prepare empowering reframes in advance. This proactive approach helps maintain positive momentum throughout the day.

Mindful Awareness Practice

Develop the habit of noticing your thoughts without judgment. This awareness creates space between stimulus and response, letting you choose more empowering interpretations.

Success Journaling

Document your reframing successes, no matter how small. This creates a powerful reference for future challenges and reinforces your ability to change limiting beliefs.

Navigating Challenges

Resistance and Setbacks

Expect internal resistance when challenging long-held beliefs. Treat setbacks as learning opportunities rather than confirmation of limiting beliefs. Each moment of awareness is progress, even if the reframe doesn't feel natural yet.

Emotional Integration

Honor the emotions behind limiting beliefs while choosing more empowering perspectives. This balance of acceptance and growth creates sustainable change.

Creating Lasting Transformation

Environmental Design

Structure your environment to support new mental scripts. Surround yourself with positive influences, inspirational materials, and reminders of your potential.

Accountability Systems

Partner with mentors or coaches who can help identify blind spots and reinforce empowering perspectives. Regular check-ins maintain momentum and provide external support.

Community Building

Connect with others on similar journeys of transformation. Share experiences, strategies, and successes to create mutual support and inspiration.

Conclusion: Your Reframing Journey

Cognitive reframing offers a powerful path to personal transformation. Through consistent practice and patience, you can reshape limiting beliefs into catalysts for growth and success. Remember this journey is uniquely yours—move at your own pace while maintaining steady progress.

Start today by choosing one limiting belief to reframe. Write it down, challenge its validity, and create an empowering alternative. Practice this new perspective consistently, celebrating small victories along the way. With each reframe, you build stronger neural pathways toward success and fulfillment.

Your mind is a powerful tool for creating positive change. By mastering cognitive reframing, you take control of your mental scripts and, ultimately, your destiny. The journey of transformation begins with a single reframe—make yours count.

Questions to ask yourself and reflect upon:

1. What stories do you tell yourself about your capabilities?
2. How do past experiences influence your current beliefs?
3. What new narratives would serve you better?
4. How do you challenge limiting stories?
5. What empowering scripts need strengthening?

CHAPTER FORTY: BUILDING PROFESSIONAL SUCCESS THROUGH INTEGRITY - A GUIDE TO ETHICAL EXCELLENCE

IN TODAY'S fast-paced professional world, success is often measured by achievements, promotions, and financial gains. However, one fundamental quality stands above all metrics: integrity. As C.S. Lewis wisely noted, "Integrity is doing the right thing, even when no one is watching."

The Foundation of Professional Integrity

Professional integrity isn't merely about following rules, it's about embodying ethical principles that guide every decision and action. Former President Dwight D. Eisenhower emphasized this when he said, "Integrity is the cornerstone of character. Without it, no real success is possible."

Let's explore the essential practices that can help you maintain unwavering integrity in your professional life:

Embrace Ethical Standards

Your professional journey should be guided by strong ethical principles. These principles serve as your moral compass, helping you navigate complex situations while staying true to your values and your organization's standards.

Champion Honesty

In an era of instant communication and information sharing, honesty has never been more important. Building trust through truthful communication creates lasting professional relationships and establishes your credibility as a reliable colleague and leader.

Protect Confidentiality

Respecting privacy and maintaining confidentiality shows professionalism and trustworthiness. This practice protects sensitive information and shows respect for others' privacy and organizational security.

Practice Transparency

Open and honest communication builds trust and fosters a positive work environment. As John D. Rockefeller Jr. stated, "Integrity is not a conditional word. It doesn't blow in the wind or change with the weather."

Uphold Fairness

A fair workplace environment requires conscious effort to treat everyone fairly and without bias. This approach promotes justice and respect while building a positive organizational culture.

Navigate Conflicts of Interest

Being aware of and properly managing potential conflicts of interest is important for maintaining professional integrity. This awareness helps prevent compromising situations and preserves your professional reputation.

The Path Forward

As Zig Ziglar pointed out, "Integrity is the foundation upon which real success is built." When faced with ethical challenges, please seek guidance from trusted mentors or colleagues. Their experience and perspective can provide valuable insights for navigating complex situations while maintaining your integrity.

Professional integrity isn't just about following rules—it's about building a sustainable foundation for long-term success. As Mahatma Gandhi reminded us, "A man is but the product of his thoughts. What he thinks, he becomes." By consistently practicing integrity, you enhance your professional reputation and contribute to creating a more ethical and positive work environment for everyone.

Questions to ask yourself and reflect upon:

1. How does integrity show up in your work?
2. When is maintaining integrity most challenging?
3. How do your actions align with your values?
4. What integrity challenges do you face?
5. How can you strengthen your professional integrity?

CHAPTER FORTY-ONE:
CULTIVATING MINDFULNESS:
A GUIDE TO LIVING FULLY
IN BOTH PERSONAL AND
PROFESSIONAL SPHERES

IN OUR FAST-PACED world where multitasking has become the norm, the practice of mindfulness offers a refreshing counterpoint. This ancient practice, rooted in being present and aware, has gained significant relevance in modern times as we seek balance in our increasingly complex lives.

The Essence of Mindfulness

At its core, mindfulness is the art of being present - observing our thoughts, feelings, and surroundings without judgment. It's not about achieving a particular state of mind, but about accepting each moment as it unfolds. As Sylvia Boorstein beautifully puts it, "Mindfulness is the aware, balanced acceptance of the present experience... opening to or receiving the present moment, pleasant or unpleasant, just as it is."

Mindfulness and Emotional Resilience

One of the most profound benefits of mindfulness is its ability to cultivate emotional resilience. By practicing mindfulness, we learn to observe our thoughts and emotions without getting caught up in them. This lets us respond to challenges with greater clarity and composure, rather than reacting impulsively.

Personal Anecdote: Barbara's Mindfulness Journey

Barbara, a high-powered executive, had always prided herself on her ability to handle stress and juggle multiple responsibilities. However, as the demands of her job grew, she found herself increasingly overwhelmed and emotionally reactive.

Seeking a solution, Barbara began practicing mindfulness meditation. At first, she struggled to quiet her racing thoughts and found the practice frustrating. But as she persisted, something began to shift.

Through mindfulness, Barbara learned to observe her stress and anxiety without judgment. She discovered that she could acknowledge these feelings without being controlled by them. This newfound awareness let her respond to challenges with greater calm and clarity.

As Barbara continued her mindfulness practice, she noticed a ripple effect in her life. She became a more patient and understanding leader, able to navigate complex situations with grace. Her relationships with colleagues and loved ones deepened as she brought greater presence and empathy to her interactions.

Mindfulness had enhanced Barbara's emotional resilience and transformed her approach to life. She had discovered a powerful tool for navigating the ups and downs of both her personal and professional worlds.

Mindfulness and Relationships

Mindfulness can profoundly impact our relationships, both personal and professional. By bringing greater presence and awareness to our interactions, we can communicate more effectively, listen more deeply, and build stronger connections.

Mindful Communication

Mindful communication involves bringing full attention to our conversations, without getting distracted by our own thoughts or agendas. It means listening to understand, rather than to respond, and expressing ourselves with clarity and compassion.

Empathy and Understanding

Mindfulness cultivates empathy by letting us set aside our own biases and see things from another's perspective. This deeper understanding can transform our relationships, fostering greater trust, collaboration, and harmony.

Presence and Connection

In our distraction-filled world, being fully present with others has become a rare gift. Mindfulness helps us offer this gift more often, creating moments of genuine connection and strengthening our bonds with others.

Mindfulness and Creativity

Mindfulness can also be a powerful tool for enhancing creativity and innovation. By quieting the mind and creating space for new ideas to emerge, mindfulness can help us break through mental blocks and access our full creative potential.

Divergent Thinking

Mindfulness promotes divergent thinking, the ability to generate multiple solutions to a problem. By observing our thoughts without judgment, we can allow ourselves to explore new possibilities and make unexpected connections.

Intuition and Insight

Mindfulness can also help us tap into our intuition and access deeper insights. By quieting the noise of our rational mind, we create space for our inner wisdom to emerge, often leading to breakthroughs and "aha" moments.

Flow States

Mindfulness can help with flow states, those moments of complete absorption in an activity where time seems to disappear. By bringing full presence to our creative pursuits, we can enter into these states more readily, enhancing both the quality and enjoyment of our work.

Nurturing Personal Mindfulness

Incorporating mindfulness into your personal life doesn't require dramatic changes. Start with these practical steps:

- Begin with brief daily meditation sessions, focusing only on your breath
- Observe your thoughts and emotions without trying to change them
- Engage in mindful activities like yoga or walking meditation
- Create technology-free periods to reduce distractions
- Practice daily gratitude reflection
- Cultivate self-compassion
- Spend time in nature regularly

Mindfulness in the Professional Sphere

The workplace presents unique opportunities to practice mindfulness:

- Take mindful breaks between tasks to reset and refocus
- Schedule regular reflection periods
- Practice single-tasking instead of multitasking
- Minimize workplace distractions
- Listen actively during conversations and meetings
- Use stress management techniques proactively
- Build meaningful professional relationships through present-moment awareness

As Jon Kabat-Zinn reminds us, "Mindfulness is a way of befriending ourselves and our experience." This friendship extends beyond personal boundaries into our professional lives, creating a harmonious blend of presence and purpose.

The Impact

When we integrate mindfulness into both personal and professional spheres, we often notice improved focus, reduced stress, better emotional regulation, and enhanced relationships. As Buddha wisely noted, "The secret of health for both mind and body is not to mourn for the past, nor to worry about the future, but to live the present moment wisely and earnestly."

Real-World Example: Google's Search Inside Yourself Program

Google, known for its innovative approach to employee well-being, developed a mindfulness-based emotional intelligence program called "Search Inside Yourself." This program, which has since been adopted by companies worldwide, teaches mindfulness techniques to enhance focus, self-awareness, and resilience.

Participants in the program have reported significant benefits, including reduced stress, improved communication, and greater creativity. Many have found that the skills learned in the program have not only enhanced their work performance but have transformed their personal lives as well.

Google's success with Search Inside Yourself demonstrates the powerful impact that mindfulness can have when integrated into the workplace. By cultivating a culture of presence and awareness, companies can create environments that foster not only productivity but also personal growth and well-being.

Mindfulness as a Way of Life

Ultimately, mindfulness is more than just a set of practices or techniques. It's a way of relating to life, a way of being fully present and engaged in each moment. By cultivating mindfulness in both our personal and professional lives, we open ourselves up to a richer, more fulfilling experience of life.

This isn't to say that mindfulness is a cure-all or that it will eliminate all of life's challenges. But it provides us with a powerful tool for navigating those challenges with greater ease and grace. It allows us to live more fully, to connect more deeply, and to find greater joy and meaning in the present moment.

Conclusion: The Lifelong Journey of Mindfulness

Mindfulness isn't about perfection - it's about practice. Each moment offers a new opportunity to begin again, to be present, and to engage with life as it unfolds.

As we continue on this lifelong journey of mindfulness, we may find that our practice evolves and deepens. What begins as a simple meditation practice may grow into a profound shift in how we relate to ourselves, others, and the world around us.

The key is to approach mindfulness with curiosity, openness, and compassion. To be patient with ourselves when our minds wander and to celebrate each moment of presence as a gift.

By cultivating mindfulness in all aspects of our lives, we open ourselves up to a world of greater clarity, connection, and joy. We discover that, even amidst the chaos and challenges of life, there is always an opportunity to find peace and purpose in the present moment.

So let us start this journey of mindfulness together, one breath, one moment at a time. As Thich Nhat Hanh reminds us, "The present moment is filled with joy and happiness. If you are attentive, you will see it." May we all learn to see and embrace the joy and happiness that is available to us in every moment.

Questions to ask yourself and reflect upon:

1. How present are you in daily activities?
2. What distracts you from the present moment?
3. How does mindfulness affect your decisions?
4. What mindfulness practices work best for you?
5. How can you bring more mindfulness to your day?

CHAPTER FORTY-TWO: DEVELOPING A GROWTH MINDSET: REFRAMING FAILURE FOR CONSISTENT PROGRESS

THE POWER of Perspective in Achievement

Success isn't merely about talent or innate ability, it's about how we interpret and respond to challenges along our journey. The difference between people who meet their goals and those who abandon them often comes down to an important factor: mindset. Understanding and developing a growth mindset can transform your relationship with failure and dramatically improve your chances of success.

Understanding Growth vs. Fixed Mindset

A growth mindset represents the belief that our abilities can be developed through dedication, learning, and persistent effort. This contrasts sharply with a fixed mindset, which views abilities as static traits that cannot be significantly changed. The implications of these different perspectives are profound and far-reaching. Research in neuroscience and psychology reveals that our brains remain plastic throughout our lives, capable of forming new neural connections and strengthening existing ones. This biological reality supports the growth mindset perspective—we can literally rewire our brains through consistent practice and learning.

People with a growth mindset typically embrace challenges as opportunities, persist in the face of setbacks, and view effort as a path to mastery. They actively learn from criticism and feedback, finding inspiration in others' success rather than feeling threatened by it. This orientation toward growth and learning creates a powerful foundation for sustained achievement.

Transforming Your Relationship with Failure

Instead of viewing failure as an endpoint or judgment of worth, a growth mindset sees it as a necessary step in the learning process. Each setback provides valuable feedback for improvement and evidence that you're pushing beyond your comfort zones. This perspective recognizes failure as a sign of courage and ambition—a temporary state rather than a permanent condition.

Think of your goals as experiments in a learning laboratory. Each attempt, successful or not, provides data to inform your next steps. This scientific perspective removes the emotional sting from failure and maintains focus on progress and discovery. By approaching challenges with curiosity rather than fear, you create space for innovation and growth.

Language and Daily Practices

The words we use shape our reality. Replace limiting phrases with growth-oriented alternatives. When you catch yourself saying "I can't," add the powerful word "yet." Transform "This is too hard" into "This requires more practice." Rather than declaring "I made a mistake," acknowledge "I found a way that doesn't work." These subtle shifts in language create profound changes in your approach to challenges.

Develop daily practices that reinforce your growth mindset. Begin each morning with reflection on growth opportunities. Engage regularly in skill-building activities that stretch your capabilities. End each day by reviewing lessons learned and expressing gratitude for the challenges you faced. Plan for growth by setting specific learning goals and identifying resources needed for development.

Building Resilience Through Support

A strong support system is crucial for maintaining a growth mindset. Surround yourself with individuals who encourage exploration and risk-taking, provide constructive feedback, and model resilient behavior. These relationships provide both emotional support and practical guidance as you navigate challenges and setbacks.

Maintain a growth journal to document your journey. Record challenges faced, lessons learned, and improvements. This practice helps find patterns in your success and struggles while providing concrete evidence of progress. Use these insights to plan next steps and celebrate the small victories along the way.

Professional and Personal Applications

Apply growth mindset principles across all areas of life. In your professional development, seek challenging assignments and ask for regular feedback. Develop new skills proactively and share your knowledge with others. Embrace industry changes as opportunities for growth rather than threats to your stability.

In personal development, push yourself to try new experiences and develop diverse interests. Build relationships that challenge and support your growth. Face fears systematically, starting with small challenges and gradually increasing difficulty. Set ambitious goals while maintaining focus on the learning process rather than just outcomes.

Managing Mindset Challenges

Recognize situations that typically trigger fixed mindset responses—high-pressure situations, public performance, competition, new environments, or technical challenges. Develop specific strategies for managing these triggers. Practice pausing to breathe and recall past successes. Focus on learning rather than immediate outcomes. Seeking support shows wisdom, not weakness.

Conclusion: Embracing the Growth Journey

Developing a growth mindset is itself a growth process, requiring patience, practice, and persistence. Begin by identifying one area where you typically maintain a fixed mindset and challenge yourself to view it through a growth lens. Notice how this shift in perspective affects your actions and outcomes.

Setbacks are not permanent defeats—they're temporary challenges on your path to mastery. Each obstacle presents an opportunity to learn, adapt, and grow stronger. Your potential is not predetermined but continuously expanding through dedicated effort and purposeful practice.

Start today by choosing one small challenge to approach with a growth mindset. Document your experience, learning, and insights. Build on this foundation day by day, watching as your capacity for growth and achievement expands. The path to success is paved with learning experiences, not perfect performances. Embrace each step of your journey, knowing that your mindset determines your ultimate destination. Your potential for growth is limitless—start exploring it today.

Questions to ask yourself and reflect upon:

1. How do you view challenges and failures?
2. What triggers a fixed mindset response?
3. How do you cultivate learning opportunities?
4. What growth experiences have shaped you most?
5. How can you strengthen your growth mindset?

CHAPTER FORTY-THREE: DISCOVER THE POWER OF YOUR CORE VALUES

HAVE you ever felt like you're going through the motions in life, without a real sense of purpose or direction? If so, it might be time to step back and explore your core values. Your core values are the guiding principles that shape your behavior, decisions, and ultimately, your destiny.

As Tony Hsieh, CEO of Zappos, wisely said, "Your personal core values define who you are, and a company's core values ultimately define the company's character and brand. For individuals, character is destiny. For organizations, culture is destiny."

When you live in alignment with your core values, you'll experience a greater sense of fulfillment and purpose. But how do you identify these values? It's a process of self-discovery, and thankfully, you've already taken the first steps by reflecting on your vision and goals.

Core values are not just a set of rules or strategies; they are the main beliefs and ethical principles that serve as your moral compass. They guide your choices, actions, and interactions with others, making sure you stay true to yourself, no matter what life throws your way.

To uncover your core values, take some time for introspection. Ask yourself, "What matters most to me? What principles do I hold dear? What beliefs guide my decisions and behaviors?" List the features that resonate with your vision, goals, and priorities.

While there's no limit to the number of core values you can have, it's best to keep your list focused and manageable – no more than five or six values. These values aren't something you simply choose; they are an authentic reflection of who you are at your core.

To get you started, here are examples of common core values:

- Authenticity, Achievement, Adventure
- Compassion, Creativity, Curiosity
- Fairness, Faith, Friendships
- Growth, Happiness, Honesty
- Kindness, Knowledge, Leadership
- Meaningful Work, Optimism, Peace
- Recognition, Respect, Responsibility
- Service, Spirituality, Success
- Trustworthiness, Wealth, Wisdom

Identifying and living by your core values is a powerful act of self-awareness and personal growth. When you align your actions with your deepest beliefs, you'll experience a profound sense of purpose and fulfillment.

So, take the time to reflect on what matters to you. Embrace your core values and let them guide you toward a life of authenticity, integrity, and lasting happiness.

Questions to ask yourself and reflect upon:

1. What values guide your most important decisions?
2. How well do your daily actions align with your values?
3. When do you feel most connected to your values?

4. What conflicts exist between different values?
5. How can you honor your values more consistently?

CHAPTER FORTY-FOUR: VISION & MISSION STATEMENTS - THE NORTH STAR OF YOUR BUSINESS SUCCESS

LET'S talk about something that's often misunderstood but crucial for your business success - vision and mission statements. I know what you're thinking: "Aren't they the same thing?" Well, let me clear that up for you!

Think of your vision statement as your North Star - that big, audacious dream you want to achieve. It's like telling yourself, "One day, I'm going to climb Mount Everest!" It's bold, inspiring, and gets your team excited about the journey ahead.

Your mission statement? That's your game plan. It's saying, "I'm going to train three hours daily, master climbing techniques, and build my endurance to reach that summit." It's practical, measurable, and most important, achievable.

Here's the key difference:

Vision = Your ultimate destination

Mission = Your roadmap to get there

Why Should You Care?

Here's something interesting: Bain and Company found that businesses that align their strategies with their vision and mission statements actually perform better. Think about it - when everyone knows where they're heading and how to get there, magic happens!

Your statements help you:

- Attract and keep top talent
- Build a motivated, dedicated team
- Foster better communication
- Make smarter decisions
- Use resources more effectively

Pro Tip: Don't just write pretty words that sound good. Your statements need teeth - they need action behind them. The best vision and mission statements are like promises you make to yourself, your team, and your customers.

Warning Signs to Watch For:

High employee turnover? Might be a sign of unclear direction

Team feeling lost? Your statements might need revisiting

Struggling with decisions? Use your statements as a compass

Remember, these statements aren't just fancy words for your website - they're your business's DNA. They help you stay focused, make better decisions, and build a team excited to come to work every day.

Ready to craft your own vision and mission statements? Keep them clear, keep them real, and most important, make them uniquely yours. They're not just statements - they're the story of where you're going and how you'll get there.

What's your business's North Star? Let's make it shine!

How to clarify your [Personal] Vision

To clarify your vision, answer these questions:

- Identify your purpose in life.
- What is your 'why'?
- What are your gifts?
- What energizes you?
- What are you passionate about?
- Know where you're going:
- How do you see yourself 5, 10, 20 years from now?
- What is your ideal future?

Determine your core values:

- What principles should you have to achieve your goals?
- What principles or standards of behavior should you learn to get there?

Questions to ask yourself and reflect upon:

1. How clear is your personal/professional vision?
2. What impact do you want to make in the world?
3. How does your mission guide daily decisions?
4. What gaps exist between vision and current reality?
5. How can you better align actions with vision?

CHAPTER FORTY-FIVE: BREAKING FREE FROM LIMITING BELIEFS - SILENCING YOUR INNER CRITIC

OUR MINDS ARE powerful architects of reality, continuously shaping our experiences through the lens of our beliefs and thought patterns. At the heart of this mental landscape lies our inner voice—a constant companion that can either lift us toward our highest potential or chain us to self-imposed limitations. Understanding and transforming this inner dialogue represents one of the most profound opportunities for personal growth and transformation.

The Nature of Limiting Beliefs

Limiting beliefs operate as silent barriers to our success and happiness, often so deeply ingrained that we mistake them for absolute truths. These beliefs typically form during our formative years, shaped by experiences, cultural messages, and significant relationships. They create a framework through which we interpret the world, influencing everything from our career choices to our personal relationships.

Common limiting beliefs manifest in thoughts like "I'm not talented enough," "Success is only for certain types of people," or "I don't deserve happiness." While these beliefs feel permanent and unchangeable, they are actually mental constructs—stories we've learned to tell ourselves that can be rewritten with conscious effort and awareness.

Understanding Your Inner Critic

The inner critic represents the voice of our limiting beliefs, often speaking with remarkable authority and conviction. This voice might have originally developed as a protective mechanism, trying to shield us from disappointment or failure. However, over time, it can become an obstacle to growth and fulfillment, keeping us trapped in patterns of self-doubt and hesitation.

To transform your relationship with your inner critic, start by developing awareness of its presence and patterns. Notice when it speaks loudest, what triggers its appearance, and the specific language it uses. This awareness creates space between you and these thoughts, letting you observe them objectively rather than accepting them as truth.

The Science of Belief Transformation

Research in neuroscience reveals that our brains have remarkable plasticity, the ability to form new neural pathways throughout our lives. This means that even long-held limiting beliefs can be transformed through consistent practice and conscious awareness. Each time we challenge a limiting belief and choose a more empowering perspective; we strengthen new neural pathways that support positive change.

Practical Strategies for Transformation

Begin by creating a belief inventory. Reflect deeply on your thoughts and find recurring patterns of self-limitation. Write these beliefs down, examining their origins and impact on your life. This process alone often reveals the arbitrary nature of many limiting beliefs.

Next, develop a practice of conscious observation. When negative self-talk arises, pause to notice it without immediate judgment. Ask yourself: "Is this thought serving my growth? What evidence exists to support or contradict this belief? What would be possible if I chose to believe something different?"

Create alternative narratives that align with your aspirations and potential. Rather than simply replacing negative thoughts with positive ones, developing nuanced, realistic perspectives that acknowledge both challenges and possibilities. For example, transform "I'm not good enough" into "I'm learning and growing every day, and my efforts contribute to my success."

Environmental Design for Belief Change

Your environment significantly influences your beliefs and thought patterns. Consciously design your surroundings to support positive change. This includes:

Creating spaces that inspire growth and possibility

Surrounding yourself with people who reflect your potential

Consuming media that reinforces empowering beliefs

Establishing routines that support self-reflection and personal development

Integration and Practice

Transforming limiting beliefs requires consistent practice and patience. Develop daily rituals that reinforce your new perspectives. This might include morning affirmations, evening reflection, or regular journaling to track your progress and insights.

Practice self-compassion throughout this process. Your limiting beliefs developed over time, often serving a protective function. Thank them for their past service while consciously choosing new, more empowering beliefs that better serve your current goals and aspirations.

Advanced Applications

As you become more skilled at identifying and transforming limiting beliefs, extend this practice into different areas of your life. Apply these principles to professional challenges, relationships, creative pursuits, and personal growth goals. Notice how changes in one area often catalyze positive shifts in others.

Maintaining Long-term Change

Sustaining belief transformation requires ongoing attention and commitment. Create systems for regular review and renewal of your mental practices. Celebrate progress while remaining vigilant for subtle ways limiting beliefs might try to reassert themselves during times of stress or challenge.

Conclusion: Your Journey Forward

Breaking free from limiting beliefs represents a profound journey of personal transformation. While the path requires courage and persistence, the rewards of living from a place of possibility rather than limitation are immeasurable. Begin today by choosing one limiting belief to examine and challenge. Each small step toward more empowering thoughts creates ripples of positive change throughout your life.

Your potential exists beyond the boundaries of your current beliefs. By consciously working to silence your inner critic and cultivate more empowering perspectives, you open yourself to extraordinary possibilities for growth, achievement, and fulfillment. The journey begins with a single thought—make it count.

Questions to ask yourself and reflect upon:

1. What beliefs most limit your potential?
2. How did these limiting beliefs develop?
3. What evidence challenges these beliefs?
4. How do limiting beliefs affect your choices?
5. What new beliefs would better serve you?

CHAPTER FORTY-SIX: THE TRANSFORMATIVE POWER OF A GROWTH MINDSET - CONTINUOUSLY EVOLVING FOR SUCCESS

IN OUR RAPIDLY EVOLVING WORLD, success and fulfillment depend increasingly on our ability to adapt, learn, and grow. The foundation of this capability lies in cultivating a growth mindset—a powerful mental framework that views abilities and intelligence not as fixed traits but as qualities that can be developed through dedication, effort, and purposeful practice.

Understanding the Growth Mindset

A growth mindset is the belief that one's abilities, intelligence, and talents can be developed and improved through effort, learning, and persistence. This perspective stands in contrast to a fixed mindset, which views these qualities as static and unchangeable.

When we embrace a growth mindset, we fundamentally transform how we approach challenges, setbacks, and opportunities. Instead of viewing our capabilities as set in stone, we recognize the vast potential for development in every area of our lives. This perspective shift creates a foundation for continuous improvement and resilience in the face of obstacles.

Example: Sarah, a software engineer, encounters a difficult coding problem. With a fixed mindset, she might think, "I'm not smart enough to solve this," and give up. However, with a growth mindset, Sarah views the challenge as an opportunity to learn and grow. She thinks, "This is a chance to expand my coding skills," and persists in finding a solution.

The Science Behind Growth Mindset

Neuroscience research confirms the brain's remarkable plasticity—its ability to form new neural connections throughout our lives. Every time we learn something new or practice a skill, our brain physically changes, creating and strengthening neural pathways. This biological reality supports the growth mindset perspective: our abilities truly can expand through dedicated effort and practice.

Core Elements of a Growth Mindset

1. **Resilience:** Resilience emerges naturally from a growth mindset. When we believe in our capacity to learn and improve, setbacks become temporary obstacles rather than permanent barriers. This resilience lets us bounce back from difficulties with renewed determination and insight.
2. **Curiosity:** Curiosity drives continuous learning and expansion. A growth mindset cultivates genuine interest in new experiences and perspectives, leading to broader knowledge and more innovative thinking. This natural curiosity creates a self-reinforcing cycle of learning and growth.
3. **Perseverance:** Perseverance becomes easier when we understand that mastery requires time and effort. Rather than expecting immediate perfection, we appreciate the journey of improvement and maintain motivation through challenges.

Practical Implementation Strategies

1. **Examine your current mindset:** Begin by examining your current mindset patterns. Notice how you respond to

challenges, criticism, and others' success. Do you see these as threats or opportunities? Your honest assessment creates a baseline for growth.

Example: Michael reflects on his reaction to a recent project setback. He realizes that he often attributes failures to a lack of innate ability. Recognizing this fixed mindset pattern, Michael commits to viewing setbacks as learning opportunities.

2. **Develop systematic learning approaches:** Develop systematic approaches to learning and improvement. Break down complex goals into manageable steps, creating clear pathways for progress. Celebrate small victories while maintaining focus on long-term development.

Example: Julia wants to improve her public speaking skills. She breaks this goal down into smaller steps, such as practicing in front of a mirror, joining a speaking group, and seeking feedback from colleagues. By focusing on incremental progress, Julia maintains motivation and builds confidence over time.

3. **Reframe challenges as growth opportunities:** Practice reframing challenges as growth opportunities. When facing difficulty, ask yourself: "What can I learn from this? How might this challenge help me develop new capabilities? What strategies haven't I tried yet?"

Example: When a major client project falls through, Amanda initially feels discouraged. However, she reframes the situation as a chance to reassess her approach and develop new strategies. By viewing the setback as a growth opportunity, Amanda maintains a positive outlook and finds innovative solutions.

Creating Growth-Oriented Environments

Your environment significantly influences your mindset development. Create spaces that encourage learning and experimentation. Surround yourself with growth-minded individuals who inspire and challenge you. Seek opportunities that stretch your capabilities while providing support for development.

Example: Robert joins a professional development group focused on leadership skills. Through discussions and workshops, he connects with growth-minded peers who share valuable insights and encourage each other's progress. This supportive environment reinforces Robert's commitment to continuous learning.

Professional Applications

In the workplace, a growth mindset transforms how we approach projects, feedback, and career development. Rather than avoiding challenging assignments, we actively seek them as opportunities for growth. Feedback becomes valuable input for improvement rather than personal criticism.

Example: As a manager, Joyce embraces a growth mindset in her leadership approach. She focuses on developing her team members' capabilities through coaching, providing stretch assignments, and encouraging experimentation. By fostering a learning-oriented culture, Joyce helps her team adapt and innovate in the face of changing business needs.

Personal Development

Apply growth mindset principles to personal goals and relationships. View personal challenges as opportunities for emotional and psychological development. Approach relationships with curiosity and openness to learning, allowing for deeper connections and mutual growth.

Example: David applies a growth mindset to his fitness journey. Instead of becoming discouraged by temporary setbacks, he views them as opportunities to refine his approach and build resilience. By embracing the learning process, David maintains motivation and achieves lasting health improvements.

Overcoming Fixed Mindset Triggers

Identify situations that typically trigger fixed mindset reactions—perhaps public speaking, receiving criticism, or facing competition. Develop specific strategies for maintaining a growth orientation in these challenging moments.

Example: Samantha recognizes that she tends to adopt a fixed mindset when receiving critical feedback on her writing. To counter this reaction, she develops a pre-feedback ritual: taking deep breaths, reminding herself of past improvements, and reframing criticism as an opportunity for growth. By proactively managing her mindset, Samantha maintains openness to learning even in challenging situations.

Advanced Growth Mindset Applications

As your growth mindset strengthens, explore more challenging applications. Take on projects outside your comfort zone, mentor others in their development journey, and seek opportunities to contribute to your field or community differently.

Example: Having cultivated a strong growth mindset, Rajesh takes on a stretch assignment at work: leading a cross-functional team to develop a new product line. Although initially daunted, Rajesh embraces the challenge as an opportunity to expand his leadership capabilities and contribute to his company's innovation efforts.

Measuring Progress

Create systems for tracking your growth journey. Document learning experiences, breakthrough moments, and lessons learned from challenges. Regular reflection helps maintain momentum and provides evidence of progress.

Example: Olivia keeps a growth mindset journal, documenting her learning experiences, reflections, and achievements. Regularly reviewing her entries, Olivia gains a clear sense of her development trajectory and identifies areas for further growth.

Sustaining Long-term Growth

Maintain your growth trajectory by regularly reviewing and updating your development goals. Stay connected with growth-minded communities and continue seeking new challenges that stretch your capabilities.

Example: Liam establishes a quarterly review process for his personal and professional growth goals. He reflects on his progress, adjusts his strategies, and sets new stretch goals for the coming months. By institutionalizing this practice, Liam sustains his growth momentum over the long term.

Conclusion: Embracing Continuous Evolution

A growth mindset opens doors to extraordinary possibilities for personal and professional development. By embracing this perspective, you position yourself for continuous learning, adaptation, and success in an ever-changing world.

Begin your growth mindset journey today by choosing one area for focused development. Each step forward, no matter how small, contributes to your overall evolution. The path to mastery is ongoing, and with a growth mindset, every experience becomes an opportunity for learning and improvement.

Your potential extends far beyond your current capabilities. By cultivating a growth mindset and applying its principles consistently, you create the foundation for continuous evolution and lasting success. Start today and watch as new possibilities unfold before you.

Questions to ask yourself and reflect upon:

1. How do you approach new challenges?
2. What role does effort play in your success?
3. How do you learn from failures?
4. What growth opportunities are you avoiding?
5. How can you strengthen your growth mindset?

CHAPTER FORTY-SEVEN: RESILIENCE MINDSET - NAVIGATING LIFE'S CHALLENGES WITH STRENGTH AND GRACE

LIFE PRESENTS us with endless challenges, from personal setbacks to professional obstacles. While we cannot control all circumstances, we can develop the mental fortitude and emotional resilience to navigate these challenges effectively. A resilience mindset empowers us to face adversity with courage, learn from setbacks, and emerge stronger from life's trials.

Understanding Resilience

Resilience isn't merely about enduring hardship, it's about adapting, growing, and even thriving in the face of adversity. This capacity for emotional and psychological adaptation represents one of humanity's most remarkable strengths. When cultivated intentionally, resilience becomes a powerful force for personal transformation and growth.

The Science of Resilience

Research in psychology and neuroscience reveals that resilience isn't a fixed trait but a set of skills and attitudes that can be developed. Our brains demonstrate remarkable adaptability in response to challenges, forming new neural pathways that support resilient responses to stress and adversity.

Core Components of Resilience

Emotional Intelligence forms the foundation of resilience. This includes the ability to recognize, understand, and manage our emotional responses to challenging situations. By developing emotional awareness, we can respond to difficulties with greater clarity and purpose.

Adaptability enables us to adjust our approaches when faced with obstacles. Rather than rigidly adhering to one solution, resilient individuals remain flexible, exploring alternative pathways and learning from each attempt.

Optimistic Realism balances positive outlook with practical assessment. This isn't blind optimism but a grounded belief in our capacity to overcome challenges while acknowledging the reality of difficulties.

Building Resilience Through Practice

Start by developing self-awareness around your response to challenges. Notice your typical reactions to stress, setbacks, and unexpected changes. This awareness creates space for choosing more resilient responses.

Practice reframing difficulties as opportunities for growth. When facing obstacles, ask yourself: "What can I learn from this? How might this challenge contribute to my development? What strengths can I develop through this experience?"

Creating Resilience-Supporting Habits

Establish daily practices that build emotional and psychological strength:

- Morning reflection to set intentions and prepare for challenges
- Regular physical exercise to build physical and mental endurance
- Mindfulness practices to develop emotional regulation
- Evening review to process experiences and extract lessons

Professional Resilience

In the workplace, resilience becomes important for long-term success. Develop strategies for managing workplace stress, adapting to change, and maintaining motivation through challenging projects. Build professional relationships that provide support and perspective during difficult times.

Personal Resilience

Apply resilience principles to personal relationships and life transitions. Develop strong support networks while maintaining healthy boundaries. Practice self-compassion during challenging times while remaining committed to growth and learning.

Advanced Resilience Strategies

As your resilience grows, explore more sophisticated approaches to managing adversity:

- **Anticipatory Planning:** Prepare for potential challenges while maintaining flexibility
- **Strategic Risk-Taking:** Push beyond comfort zones in calculated ways
- **Resilience Through Connection:** Build and maintain supportive relationships
- **Legacy Thinking:** Consider how current challenges contribute to long-term growth

Overcoming Resilience Barriers

Identify common obstacles to resilience, such as:

- Perfectionism that prevents learning from mistakes
- Fixed mindset beliefs about capabilities
- Fear of failure limiting growth opportunities
- Negative self-talk undermining confidence
- Develop specific strategies for addressing each barrier while maintaining focus on long-term development.

Measuring Resilience Growth

Track your resilience development through:

- Journal reflections on challenging experiences
- Feedback from trusted mentors and friends
- Observable changes in response to stress
- Achievement of goals despite obstacles

Sustainable Resilience Practices

Create systems for maintaining resilience over time:

- Regular assessment of coping strategies
- Ongoing skill development
- Support network maintenance
- Stress management techniques

Advanced Applications

Apply resilience principles to larger life challenges:

- Career transitions
- Major life changes
- Long-term goals
- Community leadership

Conclusion: Your Resilience Journey

Building resilience is a lifelong journey of growth and development. Each challenge presents an opportunity to strengthen your capacity for adapting and thriving in the face of adversity.

Begin today by choosing one area where you'd like to develop greater resilience. Progress often comes through small, consistent steps rather than dramatic transformations. Celebrate your growth while maintaining commitment to ongoing development.

Your capacity for resilience extends far beyond your current experience. By consciously developing this vital quality, you create the foundation for navigating life's challenges with grace, strength, and wisdom. Start your journey today, and watch as your ability to handle life's challenges transforms in remarkable ways.

The path to greater resilience begins with a single step—take that step today and begin your journey toward greater emotional strength and adaptability.

Questions to ask yourself and reflect upon:

1. How do you bounce back from setbacks?
2. What strategies help you stay resilient?
3. How do you maintain perspective during difficulties?
4. What supports your emotional recovery?
5. How can you build greater resilience?

SECTION NINE: CHAPTER SUMMARY - PERSONAL GROWTH

CHAPTER 29: The Growth Zone

- Understanding discomfort's role in growth
- Tips for recognizing and embracing discomfort
- Implementation strategies
- Success examples
- Action steps for growth

Chapters 30-31: Mindset & Authenticity

- Growth mindset cultivation
- Breaking free from limiting beliefs
- Professional applications
- Self-acceptance journey
- Action-oriented strategies

Chapters 32-33: Clarity & Positivity

- Vision and priority definition
- Unlocking potential through positivity
- Implementation framework
- Success principles
- Daily practices

Chapters 34-36: Self-Talk & Mind-Body Connection

- Transforming negative self-talk
- Understanding mind-body connection
- Professional success through integrity
- Mindfulness cultivation
- Practice strategies

Chapters 37-39: Cognitive Restructuring & Self-Awareness

- Transforming thought patterns
- Building self-awareness
- Breaking limiting beliefs
- Implementation frameworks
- Success measurements

Chapters 40-47: Advanced Personal Growth

- Professional integrity
- Mindfulness practices
- Growth mindset development
- Vision/mission clarity
- Core values identification
- Breaking limiting beliefs
- Resilience building

Key themes:

- Continuous personal development
- Practical implementation strategies
- Mind-body connection
- Success measurement
- Action-oriented approaches

SECTION TEN: STRESS REDUCTION

CHAPTER FORTY-EIGHT: FIND YOUR CALM - PRACTICAL TIPS FOR A STRESS-FREE LIFE, PERSONALLY AND PROFESSIONALLY

LET'S TALK ABOUT STRESS. It's that gnawing feeling, that constant hum of tension that many of us have become accustomed to. But what if I told you that a stress-free life, while not always perfect, is achievable? It's about making conscious choices and developing healthy habits. Fortunately, you can learn to better manage and respond to stressful situations. Let's explore tips that will guide you toward a calmer and more balanced life, both personally and professionally.

Living a Stress-Free Personal Life:

Your personal life is your sanctuary – it should be a place of peace and relaxation. Here are tips that will help you find your calm:

- **Practice Mindfulness:** Take time to focus on the present moment. Engage in activities that bring you peace and relaxation, such as meditation, yoga, or simply sitting quietly and enjoying the silence. It's about being present and fully engaging in where you are right now.
- **Exercise Regularly:** Physical activity is not just about physical health - it is amazing for mental and emotional health! Find ways to move your body that you find enjoyable – go for a

walk, take a bike ride, play a sport, or dance in your living room. It's all great for your mind.

- **Get Enough Sleep:** If you struggle to get 7 to 8 hours of quality sleep every night, put a plan into place to make that happen! Sleep is critical for your physical and mental wellbeing. Sleep deprivation exacerbates stress, so you need sleep to thrive.
- **Connect with Others:** Strong relationships provide emotional support and help reduce stress. Make it a priority to connect with friends and family. Share laughs, hugs, and meaningful experiences, so you can be reminded that you're not alone.
- **Learn to Manage Your Time:** Avoid overcommitting yourself. It's okay to say no and prioritize the most important tasks on your to-do list. Learn to create lists, plan your schedule, and stick to it to avoid feeling overwhelmed.
- **Pursue Your Passions:** Make time for activities and hobbies that bring you joy. These are essential for creating a life that's fulfilling and balanced. Don't let these slip away due to lack of time, as these activities can actually reduce your stress level and make everything feel more manageable.
- **Take Care of Yourself:** It's okay to make self-care a priority. It's not selfish - it's important! Focus on your physical, mental and emotional wellbeing and don't let these slide.
- **Learn to Say No:** Setting boundaries is essential to protecting your time and energy. Don't feel guilty about saying "no" to commitments that cause you undue stress. You have the right to manage your time.

Living a Stress-Free Professional Life:

Your work life need not feel like a constant battle. Here are tips to help you maintain calm in your professional world:

- **Prioritize and Plan:** Create a system that works for you. Make to-do lists, prioritize tasks, and break large projects down into smaller, manageable steps. This creates small successes that help to boost your confidence.

- **Practice Effective Time Management:** Avoid distractions, stay organized, and focus on the most important tasks, so you can complete your responsibilities with confidence.
- **Learn to Delegate:** Delegation can reduce your workload and improve efficiency. Don't be afraid to ask for help!
- **Take Breaks:** Regular breaks can do wonders for reducing stress and increasing focus. Get up from your desk, go for a short walk, or do something relaxing to refresh your brain.
- **Communicate Effectively:** Good communication will reduce stress and improve workplace morale. Prevent misunderstandings by using clear communication.
- **Maintain a Positive Attitude:** When you focus on the positive and keep a solution-focused mindset, the workplace environment improves and your approach to problems becomes more effective.
- **Seek Support:** Never be afraid to ask for feedback or help when needed. Colleagues can provide emotional support and a new perspective.
- **Practice Self-Care (Again!):** Self-care is essential in and out of work. Take care of your needs, so you can be effective at what you do. Schedule activities outside of work you love to do.
- **Set Realistic Goals:** Avoid overcommitting yourself and set realistic goals you know you can achieve. Don't set yourself up for failure. Instead, be realistic about what you can do, and prioritize.

Quotes to Keep You Calm and Focused:

Sometimes, we need a little inspiration to keep our stress in check. Here are a few motivational quotes that can help you live a stress-free life:

- "Stress is caused by being here but wanting to be there." - Eckhart Tolle
- "The greatest weapon against stress is our ability to choose one thought over another." - William James

- "Stress is nothing more than a socially acceptable form of mental illness." - Richard Carlson
- "Take time to do what makes your soul happy." - Unknown
- "When you can't change the direction of the wind, adjust your sails." - H. Jackson Brown Jr.
- "In the midst of movement and chaos, keep stillness inside of you." - Deepak Chopra
- "Don't let yesterday take up too much of today." - Will Rogers
- "Breathe. Let go. And remind yourself that this very moment is the only one you know you have for sure." - Oprah Winfrey
- "You can't always control what goes on outside. But you can control what goes on inside." - Wayne Dyer
- "Stressful times are opportunities to discover who you are and to grow into a better person." - Bernajoy Vaalba.

Conclusion:

Living a stress-free life is within reach, and this journey will change and evolve. By prioritizing your wellbeing, developing healthy habits, and making wise choices, you can experience more joy, balance, and fulfillment in your life and your work. Take control of your stress and find the calm within!

Questions to ask yourself and reflect upon:

1. What triggers stress in your life?
2. What practices help you find peace?
3. How do you maintain calm during chaos?
4. What boundaries need strengthening?
5. How can you create more moments of calm?

CHAPTER FORTY-NINE: MEDITATION VS CONTEMPLATION

EVER WONDERED about the difference between meditation and contemplation? Let's chat about these two fascinating practices that might seem similar at first glance but are actually distinct.

Picture meditation as hitting the pause button on your racing thoughts. It's like finding that sweet spot where you're focused on one thing - maybe your breath, a calming sound, or a meaningful phrase. You know those moments when your mind feels like a browser with 50 tabs open? Meditation helps you close those tabs and just keep one open.

Now, contemplation is more like being your own personal detective. You're diving deep into your thoughts, asking yourself the big questions, and chewing on ideas that matter to you. Think of it as having a heart-to-heart conversation with yourself, maybe writing in your journal about life's big mysteries or pondering questions without easy answers.

Here's the interesting part - while meditation is all about quieting your mental chatter, contemplation actually encourages you to think more deeply. But here's the cool thing: they're like two sides of the same coin. Both can help you feel more centered and clear-headed, in different ways.

Many people find that mixing both practices works wonders. It's like having two different tools in your mental wellness toolkit - sometimes you need the quiet of meditation, and other times you need the deep thinking of contemplation.

Practical Exercises: Meditation

Breathing Meditation

1. Find a quiet, comfortable spot where you won't be disturbed.
2. Sit comfortably, either cross-legged on a cushion or in a chair with your feet flat on the ground.
3. Close your eyes and bring your attention to your breath.
4. Notice the sensation of the air moving in and out of your nostrils, or the rise and fall of your chest.
5. When your mind wanders (and it will!), gently bring your attention back to your breath.
6. Start with just 5-10 minutes a day, gradually increasing the time as you get more comfortable.

Walking Meditation

1. Find a quiet space where you can walk comfortably, either indoors or outdoors.
2. Start walking at a natural pace, keeping your eyes open but softly focused.
3. Bring your attention to the sensations of walking - the feel of your feet hitting the ground, the movement of your legs, the swing of your arms.
4. When your mind wanders, gently bring your attention back to the sensations of walking.
5. If you're outside, you can also bring your attention to the sights, sounds, and smells around you, using them as anchors for your awareness.

Guided Meditation

1. Find a guided meditation that resonates with you. There are many free options available on YouTube or through meditation apps.
2. Find a quiet, comfortable spot where you won't be disturbed.
3. Sit or lie down comfortably and close your eyes.
4. Follow the guidance of the meditation, which may involve focusing on your breath, visualizing a peaceful scene, or repeating a mantra.
5. If your mind wanders, gently bring your attention back to the guidance.
6. Start with shorter guided meditations (5-10 minutes) and gradually work up to longer ones.

Practical Exercises: Contemplation

Journaling

1. Find a quiet spot where you can write without interruption.
2. Choose a prompt or question to contemplate. Some examples:
   ◦ What are my core values, and how do I live them out in my daily life?
   ◦ What does success mean to me, and how can I work toward it in a healthy way?
   ◦ What are the most important relationships in my life, and how can I nurture them?
3. Write freely, without worrying about grammar or punctuation. The goal is to let your thoughts flow onto the page.
4. After writing, take a few moments to read over what you've written and reflect on any insights or realizations.

Nature Contemplation

1. Find a quiet spot in nature where you can sit comfortably and observe your surroundings.

2. Take a few deep breaths and let yourself settle into the present moment.

3. Bring your attention to the details of the natural world around you - the shapes of the leaves, the texture of the bark, the sound of the birds.

4. Allow yourself to wonder and ask questions. How do the different elements of this ecosystem work together? What can nature teach me about resilience, growth, or change?

5. If insights or realizations arise, mentally note them, or write them down in a journal afterwards.

Contemplative Reading

1. Choose a book or passage that invites deep thinking and reflection. This could be a work of philosophy, a spiritual text, or even a poem.

2. Find a quiet spot where you can read without interruption.

3. Read slowly, pausing to reflect on any ideas or passages that strike you.

4. Ask yourself questions as you read. How does this idea relate to my own life and experiences? What new perspectives or insights does it offer me?

5. After reading, take a few moments to sit with your thoughts and insights. You might choose to write them down in a journal or simply sit in quiet reflection.

Scenarios: Meditation and Contemplation in Daily Life

The Busy Executive

Grace is a high-powered executive with a packed schedule and a lot of stress. She's heard that meditation can help with stress management, but she's not sure she has the time.

To start, Grace sets aside just 10 minutes each morning for a simple breathing meditation. She sits comfortably in her office chair, closes her eyes, and focuses on her breath. When thoughts of her to-do list or upcoming meetings arise, she gently brings her attention back to her breath.

After a few weeks, Grace notices she feels more centered and clear-headed throughout her workday. She's able to handle stress better and make decisions more calmly. Encouraged by these results, she decides to add a short walking meditation to her lunch break, using it as a time to reset and recharge.

The College Student

Mark is a college student grappling with big questions about his future career and life path. He's feeling overwhelmed and unsure of what direction to take.

On the advice of a mentor, Mark starts a daily journaling practice. Each evening, he sets aside 20 minutes to write about his thoughts, fears, and dreams for the future. He uses prompts like, "What are my unique strengths and passions?" and "What kind of impact do I want to make in the world?"

Through this practice, Mark starts to gain clarity on his values and goals. He realizes that he wants a career that lets him help others and make a positive difference. He also identifies some concrete steps he can take, like volunteering and taking classes in psychology, to start moving in that direction.

The Retiree

Tania is a recent retiree struggling to adjust to this new phase of life. She's feeling a loss of purpose and direction now that she's no longer working.

To help her find a new sense of meaning, Tania starts a practice of nature contemplation. Each morning, she takes a slow, mindful walk in a nearby park. She takes time to observe the changing of the seasons, the intricate details of the plants and animals, and the overall cycles of life and death in nature.

Through this practice, Tania starts to find peace in the present moment and a deeper sense of connection to the world around her. She realizes that just as nature goes through cycles of change, so too does her own life. She sees her retirement not as an ending, but as a new beginning - a chance to grow, learn, and contribute differently.

These scenarios show how meditation and contemplation can be integrated into daily life in practical, accessible ways. Whether it's a busy executive taking a few minutes to breathe, a college student using journaling to gain clarity, or a retiree finding meaning in nature, these practices can help us navigate life's challenges with greater ease and wisdom.

What's your experience with either practice? Have you tried one or both? Remember, there's no one right way to meditate or contemplate. The key is to find what works for you and make it a consistent part of your routine. Even a few minutes a day can make a big difference in your mental and emotional wellbeing.

Meditation Tips

Here are tips to help you get started with meditation:

1. **Find a quiet place:** Find a quiet and comfortable place where you can sit or lie down without being disturbed. Turn off your phone and other distractions.
2. **Set a timer:** Set a timer for the desired length of your meditation session, so you don't have to keep checking the time.
3. **Get comfortable:** Make sure you're comfortable, either sitting in a chair or lying down. You can close your eyes or keep them open, whichever feels more comfortable to you.
4. **Focus your attention:** Focus your attention on your breath, or on a mantra or word you repeat to yourself. If your mind starts to wander, simply bring your focus back to your breath or mantra.
5. **Breathe deeply:** Take deep breaths, filling your lungs and letting them expand. Exhale slowly, letting go of any tension.
6. **Be patient:** Meditation can take time to get used to, and it's

normal for your mind to wander. Don't get discouraged, just keep bringing your focus back to your breath or mantra.

7. **Gradually increase the time:** Start with a short meditation session, such as 5-10 minutes, and gradually increase the time as you get more comfortable.

8. **Make it a daily habit:** Try to make meditation a daily habit, at a time and place that works best for you.

9. **Experiment:** There are many forms of meditation, so try a few different ones and see what works best for you.

"Meditation is not a way of making your mind quiet. It's a way of entering into the quiet that's already there." - Deepak Chopra

Contemplation Tips

Here are tips to help you get started with contemplation:

1. **Find a quiet place:** Find a quiet and comfortable place where you can sit or lie down without being disturbed. Turn off your phone and other distractions.

2. **Set aside time:** Set aside dedicated time each day for contemplation, whether it be first thing in the morning or before bed at night.

3. **Get comfortable:** Make sure you're comfortable, either sitting in a chair or lying down. You can close your eyes or keep them open, whichever feels more comfortable to you.

4. **Reflect on your thoughts:** Take a moment to reflect on your thoughts, beliefs, and experiences. Ask yourself deep questions, such as"What is my purpose in life?" or"What makes me happy?"

5. **Write down your thoughts:** Consider keeping a journal where you can write down your thoughts and insights. This can help you reflect on your progress.

6. **Be open to new insights:** Be open to new insights and revelations that may come from your contemplation. The goal is not to find answers, but to gain a deeper understanding of yourself and the world around you.

7. **Be patient:** Contemplation can take time to get used to, and it's normal for your mind to wander. Don't get discouraged, just keep bringing your focus back to your thoughts and experiences.
8. **Make it a daily habit:** Try to make contemplation a daily habit, at a time and place that works best for you.
9. **Experiment:** There are many forms of contemplation, so try a few different ones and see what works best for you.

By following these tips, you can begin to experience the benefits of contemplation, including greater self-awareness, a deeper sense of purpose, and improved mental and emotional wellbeing.

"Contemplation gives you a chance to pause, catch your breath, and connect with the essence of who you are." - Tara Brach

Questions to ask yourself and reflect upon:

1. How do you currently practice reflection?
2. What benefits have you noticed from meditation?
3. How does contemplation inform your decisions?
4. What challenges arise in your practice?
5. How can you deepen your practice?

SECTION TEN: CHAPTER SUMMARY - STRESS REDUCTION

CHAPTER 48: Find Your Calm - Practical Tips for a Stress-Free Life

Personal Life Strategies:Mindfulness practice

- Regular exercise
- Adequate sleep
- Social connections
- Time management
- Self-care routines

Professional Life Strategies:

- Prioritization and planning
- Effective time management
- Delegation skills
- Regular breaks
- Clear communication
- Positive attitude maintenance

Chapter 49: Meditation vs Contemplation

Meditation Practices:

- Breathing meditation
- Walking meditation
- Guided meditation
- Implementation strategies
- Daily practice tips

Contemplation Practices:

- Journaling exercises
- Nature contemplation
- Contemplative reading
- Practical scenarios
- Integration techniques

Key differences:

- Meditation: focusing on present moment, quieting thoughts
- Contemplation: deep thinking, self-reflection, analysis

Implementation Examples:

- Busy executive scenario
- College student approach
- Retiree's practice

Common themes across chapters:

- Stress management techniques
- Practical implementation strategies
- Balance of different approaches
- Importance of consistent practice
- Personal adaptation methods

SECTION ELEVEN: SELF-CARE

CHAPTER FIFTY: MASTERING THE ART OF SELF-CARE - YOUR GUIDE TO THRIVING IN YOUR CAREER

EVER FELT like you're running on empty at work? You're not alone. In today's fast-paced professional world, self-care isn't just a luxury – it's a necessity for success. Let's talk about how you can revolutionize your work life while taking care of your most important asset: you.

The Self-Care Revolution at Work

Here's a truth bomb: You can't sprint a marathon. Yet, that's exactly what many of us try to do in our careers. We push ourselves to the limit, skip breaks, and wear "busy" like a badge of honor. But here's the game-changer – the most successful professionals aren't the ones burning the midnight oil; they're the ones who've mastered the art of self-care.

Your Self-Care Toolkit:

The Power of Pause

Break your day into sprints, not marathons. Take those 5-minute walks. Step away from your desk. Your productivity will thank you.

Boundaries Are Your Best Friend

"No" is a complete sentence. Set clear work hours and stick to them. Your emails will still be there tomorrow.

Stress-Proof Your Workday

Deep breathing, mindfulness, or a quick stretch – find your stress-busting ritual and make it non-negotiable.

Warren Buffett said: "The best investment you can make is in your own abilities." Think of self-care as compound interest for your career – small, consistent investments yield remarkable returns.

Action Steps:

1. **Take breaks:** Set aside time for short breaks during the day, such as stretching or taking a walk, to refresh your mind and body.
2. **Set boundaries:** Establish clear boundaries between work and personal time to reduce stress and prevent burnout.
3. **Manage stress:** Practice stress management techniques, such as deep breathing, mindfulness, or physical exercise, to help you stay calm and focused at work.
4. **Prioritize self-care:** Make self-care a priority and set aside time each day for activities that help you recharge and unwind.
5. **Network and collaborate:** Connect with colleagues and join team building activities to improve relationships and boost morale in the workplace.
6. **Set realistic goals:** Set achievable goals and prioritize your tasks to manage your workload and reduce stress.
7. **Speak up:** Communicate your needs and boundaries assertively and seek support from your colleagues and supervisor when needed.
8. **Pursue professional development:** Invest in your career by attending training and workshops, seeking mentorship, or taking courses to improve your skills and knowledge.
9. **Celebrate successes:** Take time to acknowledge and appreciate

your accomplishments and celebrate the successes of your colleagues.

10. **Maintain work-life balance:** Establish a healthy balance between work and personal life and avoid sacrificing one for the other.

Questions to ask yourself and reflect upon:

1. What does effective self-care look like for you?
2. How do you prioritize your wellbeing?
3. What self-care practices need more attention?
4. What barriers prevent consistent self-care?
5. How can you make self-care more sustainable?

CHAPTER FIFTY-ONE:
POWER OF PERSPECTIVE -
REFRAMING STRESS FOR
SUCCESS AND GROWTH

STRESS IS OFTEN SEEN as the villain in our personal and professional lives. We blame it for our sleepless nights, our shortened tempers, and our lack of joy. But what if we've been looking at stress all wrong? What if, instead of trying to eliminate stress, we could harness its power to fuel our growth and success? Welcome to the transformative art of reframing stress.

The Science of Stress Reappraisal

Research in psychology and neuroscience is uncovering a fascinating truth: our mindset about stress matters more than the stress itself. When we view stress as a threat, our body's fight-or-flight response kicks in, leading to all those familiar negative symptoms. But when we see stress as a challenge, an opportunity for growth, something remarkable happens.

Reframing Stress in Action:

Stress as a Sign of Meaning

That knot in your stomach before a big presentation? It's a sign that you care about doing well. Your stress is a signal this matters to you. Reframe stress as a marker of meaning, and let it energize your efforts.

Stress as a Catalyst for Growth

Think about a time you overcame a stressful challenge. Did you emerge stronger, wiser, more resilient? Stress can be the resistance we need to grow our capabilities. Embrace stress as your training ground for personal and professional development.

Stress as a Connection Enhancer

Stressful experiences, when shared, can be powerful bonding moments. Reaching out to others in times of stress cultivates empathy, trust, and a sense of "we're in this together." Let stress remind you of your shared humanity and the support available to you.

Stress as a Prioritizing Tool

When everything feels urgent and important, stress can be a clarifying force. It nudges us to get crystal clear on our values and priorities. Let stress sharpen your focus on what matters and let the rest fall away.

Putting Reappraisal into Practice:

1. **Notice your stress narrative.** When you feel stressed, pause and observe your thoughts. Are you telling yourself a story of threat or opportunity?
2. **Question your stress assumptions.** Challenge the belief that stress is inherently bad. Look for counterexamples where stress fueled your best work or most meaningful connections.
3. **Reframe your stress response.** When you notice stress symptoms, reinterpret them. See racing heart as your body preparing for action. View sweaty palms as a sign that you're alive and engaged.
4. **Share your stress.** Contact a trusted colleague, friend, or family member. Express how you're feeling and ask for their perspective. Collaborative problem solving can turn stress into connection.
5. **Reflect and grow.** After a stressful event, take time to reflect. What did you learn about yourself, your values, your strengths? How can you apply these insights moving forward?

Stress Reappraisal Mantras:

- "This stress means I'm growing."
- "Pressure is privilege." - Billie Jean King
- "Stress is my body rising to this challenge."
- "I can handle this."
- "This stress will pass but my growth will last."

Conclusion: Your Stress, Your Power

Stress isn't going away. It's an inevitable part of lives rich with meaning and challenge. By changing our relationship to stress, we can transform it from an obstacle to an ally.

Every time you reframe a stressful moment; you're rewiring your brain's response. You're creating a new pattern, a new habit of resilience and growth. This is the power of stress reappraisal - the power to turn your greatest challenges into your greatest opportunities.

So the next time stress comes knocking, take a deep breath, remember your reframe, and open the door. Greet stress as a familiar friend, here to remind you of your values, your strength, and your ability to handle whatever comes your way. This is stress on your terms, stress in service of the life and career you're creating.

You have the power to author your own stress story. Make it one of meaning, growth, and unstoppable resilience. Your stressful moments are waiting to be transformed - are you ready to begin?

Questions to ask yourself and reflect upon:

1. How do different perspectives affect your experiences?
2. When do you struggle to maintain perspective?
3. How do you seek new viewpoints?
4. What helps you shift perspective?
5. How can you broaden your perspective?

CHAPTER FIFTY-TWO: THE ART OF SELF-CARE - YOUR GUIDE TO A MORE FULFILLED LIFE

LET'S have a heart-to-heart about something we often push to the bottom of our to-do lists: self-care. No, it's not just about fancy spa days or expensive retreats – it's about making conscious choices that nurture your mind, body, and soul.

You know that feeling when your phone's battery is running low? That's exactly how we function when we're running on empty. Just as you wouldn't let your phone die, you shouldn't let yourself run out of juice either!

The Self-Care Revolution Starts With You

Think of self-care as your personal investment portfolio – except instead of stocks and bonds, you're investing in your wellbeing. Warren Buffett once said, "The best investment you can make is in your own abilities." And boy, was he right!

Here's your starter pack for self-care success:

Sleep Like You Mean It

Your body needs that reset button! Aim for 7-9 hours of quality sleep. Create a bedtime ritual that signals your brain it's time to wind down.

Fuel Your Machine

Nourish your body with whole foods that make you feel energized. Remember, you're eating for energy, not just taste (though who says healthy can't be delicious?).

Move That Beautiful Body

Exercise doesn't mean running marathons. Find your joy in movement – dance in your living room, take a peaceful walk, or stretch like a cat. Your body will thank you!

The Mental Game

Let's talk about the game-changer: mental self-care. As Lalah Delia wisely put it, "Self-care is how you take your power back." Practice mindfulness, set boundaries with your digital devices, and make time for activities that light up your soul.

Action Steps:

1. **Prioritize sleep:** Get enough sleep each night to help you feel refreshed and rejuvenated.
2. **Eat a healthy diet:** Consume a balanced diet rich in whole foods, fruits, and vegetables to maintain good physical and mental health.
3. **Exercise regularly:** Engage in physical activity, such as going for a walk, running, or practicing yoga, to improve your physical and mental wellbeing.
4. **Manage stress:** Engage in activities that help you manage stress, such as meditation, deep breathing, or yoga.
5. **Practice self-reflection:** Take time to reflect on your thoughts and emotions, and practice self-compassion and kindness toward yourself.
6. **Connect with others:** Spend time with loved ones and engage in social activities to strengthen relationships and boost your mood.
7. **Take breaks:** Set aside time for relaxation and leisure activities,

such as reading, watching a movie, or taking a bath, to help you recharge and unwind.

8. **Practice mindfulness**: Focus on the present moment and pay attention to your thoughts, feelings, and sensations without judgment.

9. **Limit screen time:** Reduce the time you spend on screens, such as your phone, computer, or TV, to improve your mental health and wellbeing.

10. **Engage in self-care activities:** Engage in activities you enjoy and that bring you joy and fulfillment, such as playing a musical instrument, painting, or gardening.

Questions to ask yourself and reflect upon:

1. What nurtures you physically, mentally, and emotionally?
2. How do you recognize when you need self-care?
3. What self-care practices are most effective?
4. How do you maintain boundaries around self-care?
5. What would enhance your self-care routine?

CHAPTER FIFTY-THREE: SELF-CARE IS NOT SELFISH - PRIORITIZING YOUR WELLBEING FOR A BETTER LIFE

LET'S have a heart-to-heart about something we often push to the bottom of our to-do lists: self-care. No, it's not just about fancy spa days or expensive retreats – it's about making conscious choices that nurture your mind, body, and soul.

You know that feeling when your phone's battery is running low? That's exactly how we function when we're running on empty. Just as you wouldn't let your phone die, you shouldn't let yourself run out of juice either!

The Self-Care Revolution Starts With You

Think of self-care as your personal investment portfolio – except instead of stocks and bonds, you're investing in your wellbeing. Warren Buffett once said, "The best investment you can make is in your own abilities." And boy, was he right!

Here's your starter pack for self-care success:

Sleep Like You Mean It

Your body needs that reset button! Aim for 7-9 hours of quality sleep. Create a bedtime ritual that signals your brain it's time to wind down.

Fuel Your Machine

Nourish your body with whole foods that make you feel energized. Remember, you're eating for energy, not just taste (though who says healthy can't be delicious?).

Move That Beautiful Body

Exercise doesn't mean running marathons. Find your joy in movement – dance in your living room, take a peaceful walk, or stretch like a cat. Your body will thank you!

The Mental Game

Let's talk about the game-changer: mental self-care. As Lalah Delia wisely put it, "Self-care is how you take your power back." Practice mindfulness, set boundaries with your digital devices, and make time for activities that light up your soul.

Action Steps:

1. **Prioritize sleep:** Get enough sleep each night to help you feel refreshed and rejuvenated.
2. **Eat a healthy diet:** Consume a balanced diet rich in whole foods, fruits, and vegetables to maintain good physical and mental health.
3. **Exercise regularly:** Engage in physical activity, such as going for a walk, running, or practicing yoga, to improve your physical and mental wellbeing.
4. **Manage stress:** Engage in activities that help you manage stress, such as meditation, deep breathing, or yoga.
5. **Practice self-reflection:** Take time to reflect on your thoughts and emotions, and practice self-compassion and kindness toward yourself.
6. **Connect with others:** Spend time with loved ones and engage in social activities to strengthen relationships and boost your mood.
7. **Take breaks:** Set aside time for relaxation and leisure activities, such as reading, watching a movie, or taking a bath, to help

you recharge and unwind.

8. **Practice mindfulness**: Focus on the present moment and pay attention to your thoughts, feelings, and sensations without judgment.

9. **Limit screen time:** Reduce the time you spend on screens, such as your phone, computer, or TV, to improve your mental health and wellbeing.

10. **Engage in self-care activities:** Engage in activities you enjoy and that bring you joy and fulfillment, such as playing a musical instrument, painting, or gardening.

Questions to ask yourself and reflect upon:

1. What beliefs do you hold about self-care?
2. How does self-care affect your relationships?
3. When do you feel guilty about self-care?
4. How does self-care impact your effectiveness?
5. What permission do you need to give yourself?

SECTION ELEVEN: CHAPTER SUMMARY - SELF-CARE

CHAPTER 50: Mastering the Art of Self-Care - Your Guide to Thriving in Your Career

- Self-care revolution at work
- Professional self-care toolkit:
- Power of pause
- Boundary setting
- Stress-proofing strategies
- Action steps for workplace implementation
- Work-life balance maintenance

Chapter 51: Power of Perspective - Reframing Stress

- Science of stress reappraisal
- Reframing strategies:
  - Stress as meaning
  - Stress as growth catalyst
  - Stress as connection enhancer

- Stress as prioritizing tool
- Practical implementation steps
- Stress reappraisal mantras

Chapter 52-53: The Art of Self-Care & Self-Care is Not Selfish

- Fundamental self-care practices:
  - Sleep optimization
  - Proper nutrition
  - Physical movement
  - Mental wellbeing
- Implementation strategies:
  - Daily practices
  - Boundary setting
  - Stress management
  - Mindfulness cultivation

Key themes across chapters:

- Self-care as necessity
- Practical implementation strategies
- Balance of physical and mental wellbeing
- Stress management techniques
- Boundary setting importance

SECTION TWELVE: TAKING ACTION:

CHAPTER FIFTY-FOUR: THE POWER OF CONSISTENT ACTION - YOUR BRIDGE FROM DREAMS TO REALITY

THE DISTANCE between dreams and achievement is bridged by one fundamental element: consistent action. While many of us harbor grand visions and aspirations, it's the steady rhythm of daily progress that transforms these dreams into tangible results. Understanding and harnessing the transformative power of consistency creates lasting change and meaningful achievement in your life.

Understanding the Power of Consistency

Every significant achievement in human history began with a single step, followed by countless others. Whether it's building a successful business, mastering a craft, or transforming your health, the foundation of achievement lies not in sporadic bursts of effort but in the steady accumulation of purposeful actions. This principle holds true across all domains of human endeavor, from artistic creation to scientific discovery.

The Psychology of Consistent Action

When we take consistent action, we create powerful neural pathways that support our goals. Each small step reinforces our commitment and builds momentum, making subsequent actions easier and more natural. This neurological reinforcement transforms challenging behaviors into automatic habits, creating a self-sustaining cycle of progress and achievement.

The brain responds to consistent patterns by strengthening neural connections related to specific behaviors. Over time, these strengthened pathways make it easier to maintain positive habits and continue taking action toward our goals, even when motivation temporarily wanes.

Starting Your Journey

Begin by identifying one compelling goal that energizes you. Rather than becoming overwhelmed by the magnitude of your ambition, break it down into the smallest possible daily actions. Commit to just 10-15 minutes of focused effort each day, understanding these minor investments accumulate into significant progress over time.

Success requires creating structured systems that support consistent action. Establish a morning routine that primes you for productivity and achievement. Develop simple methods for tracking your progress, implementing regular review periods to assess and adjust your approach. Most importantly, design your environment to minimize friction and support your desired behaviors.

Navigating Challenges

Resistance is a natural part of any growth process. Rather than viewing it as an obstacle, recognize discomfort as a sign that you're pushing beyond your current limitations. Prepare strategies for handling common obstacles, maintaining focus during challenging periods, and building resilience through gradual progression.

Success requires staying power, particularly when facing inevitable setbacks. Rather than seeking perfection, focus on maintaining forward momentum. Develop quick recovery strategies for when you temporarily veer off course and celebrate small victories along the way. These celebrations reinforce positive behaviors and maintain motivation during challenging periods.

Building Your Support Network

Creating a strong support network proves crucial for sustaining long-term effort. Connect with accountability partners who understand and support your goals. Join communities of like-minded individuals pursuing similar objectives. Seek guidance from experienced mentors who can provide valuable insights and perspective. Share your journey with others, understanding that your experience might inspire their own growth.

The Hidden Power of Small Actions

The true magic of consistent action often lies in its mundanity. Major transformations rarely happen through dramatic gestures but through the patient accumulation of small improvements. Trust in this process, recognizing that significant changes often seem minor in the moment but compound powerfully over time.

Creating Sustainable Systems

Develop daily practices that support your goals through specific time blocks for key actions and clear triggers for desired behaviors. Review your progress regularly, adjusting your approach based on what you learn. Weekly planning sessions help you anticipate challenges and prepare accordingly, while monthly assessments provide opportunities to evaluate overall progress and refine your strategies.

Advanced Implementation

As you build momentum, explore more sophisticated approaches to maintaining consistency. Create systems that stack complementary habits, automate routine decisions, and build in multiple layers of accountability. Develop contingency plans for managing disruptions while maintaining progress toward your goals.

Measuring and Sustaining Progress

Document your journey through detailed progress logs and key lessons. Note pattern changes and breakthrough moments, using these insights to refine your approach. Regular goal review and adjustment ensure your actions remain aligned with your evolving aspirations.

Continuous skill development and support network maintenance provide the foundation for ongoing growth.

Conclusion: Your Journey Forward

The path to achievement isn't about dramatic transformations but the power of persistent, focused effort. Begin today by selecting one meaningful goal and identifying the smallest possible action you can take toward it. Commit to this action daily, knowing that each step builds momentum toward your larger vision.

Consistency trumps intensity. Small actions performed reliably create more lasting change than occasional heroic efforts. Your success builds on the foundation of today's choices and actions, however modest they might seem.

Start now with whatever resources you have available. Choose one tiny action that moves you toward your goals and commit to performing it today. Then repeat tomorrow. Your future self will thank you for the consistency you begin today. The journey of a thousand miles begins with a single step, but it's the consistent steps that follow that ensure you reach your destination.

Questions to ask yourself and reflect upon:

1. How consistent are you in pursuing goals?
2. What helps you maintain momentum?
3. What disrupts your consistency?
4. How do you rebuild after interruptions?
5. What systems support consistent action?

CHAPTER FIFTY-FIVE: THE PROCRASTINATION KILLER - ESSENTIAL MINDSET SHIFTS TO START TAKING ACTION

PROCRASTINATION STANDS as one of the most formidable barriers between us and our aspirations. We've all experienced those moments of paralysis - staring at our to-do list while our precious time slips away into the void of social media scrolling or Netflix binges. Yet procrastination isn't an immutable character trait; it's a pattern of behavior that can be transformed through strategic mindset shifts and practical techniques.

Understanding the Psychology of Procrastination

At its core, procrastination represents a disconnect between our present and future selves. We focus on immediate comfort over long-term benefits, often driven by underlying fears, perfectionism, or over-whelm. Understanding these psychological dynamics proves crucial for breaking free from procrastination's grip.

The human brain naturally seeks pleasure and avoids pain. When we perceive tasks as challenging or uncomfortable, our instinct pushes us toward easier, more immediately rewarding activities. However, this short-term comfort comes at the cost of our longer-term goals and aspirations.

Transformative Mindset Shifts

The Growth Perspective

Cultivating a growth mindset fundamentally transforms how we approach challenges. Instead of viewing difficulties as threats to avoid, we see them as opportunities for development and learning. This shift helps dissolve the fear and resistance that often fuel procrastination.

When facing a challenging task, rather than focusing on potential failure, ask yourself: "What can I learn from this experience? How will tackling this challenge help me grow?" This perspective makes starting easier and builds momentum through small victories.

Long-Term Vision Over Immediate Comfort

Developing a compelling long-term vision creates a powerful antidote to procrastination. By vividly imagining and connecting with the future benefits of our actions, we strengthen our motivation to overcome temporary discomfort.

Take time to clearly visualize how meeting your goals will transform your life. Create detailed mental pictures of the positive changes you'll experience. Make this future vision so compelling that it outweighs the temporary pleasure of procrastination.

Embracing Imperfect Progress

Perfectionism often masquerades as high standards but actually serves as a sophisticated form of procrastination. Breaking free requires embracing the power of imperfect action and understanding that progress trumps perfection.

Start viewing your work as iterations rather than final products. Each action, however imperfect, moves you closer to your goals and provides valuable feedback for improvement. Remember: done is better than perfect, and action breeds clarity.

The Power of Self-Compassion

Harsh self-criticism about procrastination often creates a negative feedback loop, leading to more avoidance behavior. Cultivating self-compassion breaks this cycle, creating space for positive change and growth.

Practice treating yourself with the same kindness you'd offer a friend struggling with similar challenges. Acknowledge your efforts, learn from setbacks, and maintain a supportive inner dialogue that encourages continued progress.

Time as a Finite Resource

Developing a healthy awareness of time's finite nature can dramatically shift how we approach our goals and priorities. When we internalize that time is our most precious and non-renewable resource, we naturally become more intentional about its use.

Practical Implementation Strategies

The Power Hour Technique

Dedicate one focused hour each day to your most important goal. During this time, eliminate all distractions and work with single-minded purpose. This builds momentum and proves that you can make significant progress in relatively short time blocks.

Progressive Task Breakdown

Break larger projects into smaller, manageable parts. Create detailed action steps that feel achievable rather than overwhelming. This approach makes starting easier and provides clear markers of progress.

Environment Design

Shape your physical and digital environment to support focused action. Remove common distractions, create dedicated workspaces, and use tools that enhance rather than hinder productivity.

Building Momentum Through Small Wins

Start each day with a small but meaningful task related to your goals. These early wins create positive momentum that can carry through the entire day. Celebrate these small victories while maintaining focus on larger goals.

Creating Accountability Systems

Establish external accountability through partners, mentors, or group commitments. Share your goals and progress regularly, creating social pressure that supports consistent action.

Advanced Strategies for Sustained Change

Identity-Based Transformation

Work on shifting your core identity from someone who procrastinates to someone who takes consistent action. This deeper transformation supports lasting behavioral change.

Energy Management

Align your most important tasks with your peak energy periods. Understanding and working with your natural rhythms enhances productivity and reduces resistance.

Conclusion: Your Action Journey

Overcoming procrastination requires more than just willpower or time management techniques. It demands a fundamental shift in how we think about challenges, progress, and our relationship with time.

Begin today by choosing one important task you've been avoiding. Apply these mindset shifts and strategies to take your first step forward. Transformation happens through consistent small actions, not dramatic overnight changes.

Your success depends on the actions you take today. Don't let procrastination continue stealing your dreams. With these mindset shifts and practical strategies, you can become the consistent action-taker you're meant to be. Start now - your future self will thank you for it.

Questions to ask yourself and reflect upon:

1. What tasks do you typically procrastinate on?
2. What triggers your procrastination?

3. How do you overcome procrastination?
4. What strategies work best for you?
5. How can you prevent procrastination?

CHAPTER FIFTY-SIX: TRANSFORM YOUR DREAMS INTO REALITY - THE POWER OF PERSONAL ACTION LISTS

EVER FELT OVERWHELMED by your goals and dreams? You're not alone. Today, turning aspirations into achievements can seem like climbing Mount Everest. But here's the game-changer: creating a personal action list. As Abraham Lincoln wisely said, "The best way to predict the future is to create it."

Let's Get Real About Action Lists

Think of your action list as your personal GPS to success. It's not just another to-do list – it's your roadmap to turning those "someday" dreams into "done that" victories. The beauty of it? You don't need fancy tools or complex systems to start. As Martin Luther King Jr. reminded us, "You don't have to see the whole staircase, just take the first step."

Your 7-Step Success Formula:

Dream Big, Plan Smart

Start by setting crystal-clear goals. Want to run a marathon? Great! But first, can you run a mile? Remember, specific and measurable goals are your best friends.

Chunk It Down

Break those mighty goals into bite-sized pieces. Running a marathon? Start with choosing your running shoes. Small steps lead to big victories.

Play Priority Tetris

Not all tasks are created equal. Prioritize like a pro – what moves the needle most? Focus there first.

Time Is Your Ally

Give each task a deadline. As Karen Lamb puts it, "A year from now, you'll wish you had started today." Make that timeline realistic but challenging.

Find Your Flow

Whether you're a digital warrior or a paper-and-pen enthusiast, choose a tracking system that feels natural to you. The best system? The one you'll actually use.

Keep It Fresh

Regular reviews keep your list relevant and your motivation high. Think of it as your personal success check-in.

Victory Dance Time

Celebrate every win, no matter how small. As Oprah Winfrey says, focus on significance, not just success. Those small victories? They're building your success story.

The Magic Formula

Antoine de Saint-Exupery nailed it: "A goal without a plan is just a wish." Your action list transforms those wishes into concrete steps. And remember Anatole France's wisdom: success requires both dreaming AND doing.

Ready to transform your life? Start your action list today. Because your future self will thank you for the steps you take right now.

Questions to ask yourself and reflect upon:

1. What dreams need concrete action plans?
2. How do you break down big goals?
3. What support systems do you need?
4. How do you maintain motivation?
5. What's your next actionable step?

CHAPTER FIFTY-SEVEN: CLIMB YOUR CAREER LADDER - THE STRATEGIC POWER OF PROFESSIONAL ACTION LISTS

READY TO TAKE your career from cruising to soaring? Let's talk about the secret weapon successful professionals use to climb the corporate ladder: the career action list. When career paths are more like jungle gyms than ladders, staying organized isn't just helpful – it's essential.

Blueprint for Professional Excellence

Think of your career action list as your professional GPS. It's not about mapping every turn of your career journey; it's about knowing your next three moves while keeping your ultimate destination in sight. Whether you're gunning for that corner office or dreaming of launching your own empire, your action list is your battle plan.

Seven Steps to Career Mastery:

1. **Dream with Deadlines**

Vague goals like "get promoted" won't cut it. Instead, try "complete leadership certification by Q3" or "increase team productivity by 25% within six months." Make your goals as specific as a coffee order at your favorite café.

2. Slice the Elephant

Remember the old question: How do you eat an elephant? One bite at a time. That big career goal? Break it down into weekly or daily tasks. Want to become a department head? Start by mastering your current role, then identify skill gaps, network strategically, and so on.

3. Master the Art of Priority

Not all tasks are created equal. Use the "impact vs. effort" matrix. High impact, low effort? Do it now. Low impact, high effort? Maybe that can wait.

4. Time Block Like a Pro

Your calendar is your best friend. Block time for career development like you would for important meetings. Treat your goals with the same respect you give your clients.

5. Find Your Productivity Groove

Maybe you're a Trello master, or maybe good old pen and paper is your jam. Choose a system that feels as natural as your morning coffee routine.

6. Regular Reality Checks

Schedule monthly career check-ins with yourself. Are your goals still aligned with market trends? Is your industry shifting? Adapt accordingly.

7. Toast Your Wins

Land a new client? Nail that presentation? Master a new skill? Celebrate! Success breeds success and acknowledging your progress fuels motivation for the next challenge.

The Career Catalyst

Your action list isn't just a to-do list – it's your career catalyst. It transforms vague professional dreams into concrete achievements. Career success rarely happens by accident. It's the result of deliberate planning and consistent action.

Your Next Move

Start today. Pull out your notebook, open your favorite app, or grab that whiteboard marker. Map out your professional journey one action item at a time. Your future self will thank you for the clarity and direction you're creating right now.

Questions to ask yourself and reflect upon:

1. What's your next career milestone?
2. How are you preparing for advancement?
3. What skills need development?
4. How do you create opportunities?
5. What support do you need?

SECTION TWELVE: CHAPTER SUMMARY - TAKING ACTION

Chapter 54: The Power of Consistent Action

- Understanding consistency's role
- Psychology of consistent action
- Starting your journey
- Building support networks
- Creating sustainable systems
- Measuring progress

Chapter 55: The Procrastination KillerPsychology of procrastination

- Transformative mindset shifts:
  - Growth perspective
  - Long-term vision
  - Embracing imperfect progress
  - Self-compassion
- Practical implementation strategies
- Advanced strategies for change

. . .

Chapter 56: Transform Your Dreams into Reality

7-Step Success Formula:

- Dream big, plan smart
- Chunk it down
- Priority management
- Time allocation
- System selection
- Regular reviews
- Celebration of wins

Chapter 57: Climb Your Career Ladder

- Professional action lists
- Seven steps to career mastery:
  - Specific goal setting
  - Task breakdown
  - Priority management
  - Time blocking
  - System optimization
  - Regular reviews
  - Success celebration

Key themes across chapters:

- Consistent action importance
- Strategic implementation
- Progress measurement
- Support system development
- Regular review processes

SECTION THIRTEEN: TIME MANAGEMENT

CHAPTER FIFTY-EIGHT: THE LIFE-CHANGING MAGIC OF TIME BLOCKING - HOW TO MULTIPLY YOUR OUTPUT

IN OUR HYPERCONNECTED WORLD, the constant barrage of notifications, requests, and responsibilities can leave us feeling perpetually overwhelmed and scattered. Despite working longer hours, many of us end each day wondering what we actually accomplished. The solution lies not in working harder, but in working smarter through the transformative practice of time blocking.

Understanding the Time Management Crisis

Modern work culture celebrates multitasking and constant availability, yet research consistently shows these practices dramatically reduce our effectiveness and satisfaction. Each context switch costs valuable mental energy and focus, while reactive work patterns keep us stuck in a cycle of busy work rather than meaningful progress.

The cost of this scattered approach extends beyond mere productivity. It affects our stress levels, creativity, and ability to achieve deep work on complex projects. Most importantly, it robs us of the satisfaction that comes from making consistent progress toward our most important goals.

The Time Blocking Revolution

Time blocking represents a fundamental shift from reactive to proactive time management. Instead of letting your schedule be dictated by incoming demands, you consciously designate specific time periods for your highest-priority work. This simple yet powerful approach creates the space needed for focused, meaningful progress on what matters most.

The Science Behind Time Blocking

Research in cognitive psychology reveals that our brains perform best when focused on a single task or type of work. Time blocking aligns with this natural tendency, letting us harness our peak mental energy for our most important work. By reducing context switching and decision fatigue, we preserve cognitive resources for creative and strategic thinking.

Core Principles of Effective Time Blocking

Priority Alignment

Begin by clearly identifying your highest-leverage activities - those tasks that move the needle toward your most important goals. These become your primary candidates for dedicated time blocks. Think carefully about when you have the most energy and focus, reserving these periods for your most challenging and important work.

Block Architecture

Create blocks of 60-180 minutes, recognizing that meaningful progress often requires sustained attention. Consider your natural energy rhythms when scheduling these blocks. Many find their peak cognitive hours occur in the morning, making this an ideal time for complex or creative work.

Protection Protocols

Treat your time blocks as sacred appointments with yourself. Develop systems to reduce interruptions during these periods - turn off notifications, find a quiet space to work, and communicate your unavailability to others. The effectiveness of time blocking depends largely on your ability to maintain these boundaries.

Buffer Management

Build flexibility into your schedule by including buffer blocks for unexpected tasks and opportunities. This prevents your carefully planned schedule from derailing when surprises inevitably arise.

Implementation Strategies

Starting Simple

Begin with just one or two important time blocks per day. Focus on protecting these periods and using them effectively before expanding your practice. Success with even limited time blocking can create dramatic improvements in your productivity and satisfaction.

Calendar Integration

Use your calendar as a proactive planning tool rather than a recording of commitments. Block off your focus time first, then work other commitments around these protected periods. This ensures your highest priorities receive the attention they deserve.

Environment Design

Create physical and digital environments that support focused work during your time blocks. This might include:

- A dedicated workspace free from distractions
- Specific tools or resources needed for deep work
- Clear signals to others about your unavailability
- Digital tools configured to reduce interruptions

Advanced Time Blocking Techniques

Theme Days

Designate entire days for specific types of work or projects. This approach can be particularly effective for creative or strategic work that benefits from extended focus.

Energy Mapping

Track your energy levels throughout the day and week to optimize your block scheduling. Align your most demanding tasks with your peak energy periods for maximum effectiveness.

Iterative Refinement

Regularly review and adjust your time blocking strategy. What works today may need changes as your responsibilities and goals evolve. Maintain flexibility while preserving the core principle of protected focus time.

Measuring Success

Track both quantitative and qualitative metrics:

- Project completion rates
- Quality of work produced
- Stress levels and satisfaction
- Progress toward key goals

Overcoming Common Challenges

Interruption Management

Develop specific strategies for handling various types of interruptions without derailing your focused work. This might include designated check-in times or clear communication protocols for urgent matters.

Adaptation Strategies

Create contingency plans for when your time blocks get disrupted. Having predetermined responses helps maintain momentum even when perfect adherence isn't possible.

Conclusion: Your Time Mastery Journey

Time blocking represents more than just a productivity technique - it's a fundamental shift in how you approach your time and energy. By proactively designing your days around your highest priorities, you create the conditions for exceptional output and satisfaction.

Begin today by identifying an important priority and scheduling a protected block of time for focused work on this goal. Start small but start now. With consistent practice, you'll discover the transformative power of working with your natural rhythms rather than against them.

Your time is your most precious resource. Through thoughtful time blocking, you can ensure it's invested in what matters, creating the results and impact you're capable of achieving.

Questions to ask yourself and reflect upon:

1. How effectively do you manage your time?
2. What time management tools work best?
3. How do you prioritize tasks?
4. What time wasters need elimination?
5. How can you improve productivity?

CHAPTER FIFTY-NINE: MODERN TIME MASTERY - DIGITAL TOOLS AND TEAM PRODUCTIVITY

The Digital Revolution in Time Management

Let's face it - the way we work has completely transformed. Gone are the days of simple to-do lists and desk calendars. In today's fast-paced digital world, we need to embrace a whole new approach to managing our time and energy. Whether you're working remotely, collaborating across time zones, or juggling multiple digital platforms, mastering modern time management is crucial for your success.

Building Your Digital Command Center

Think of your digital productivity system as your personal command center. Just like a well-designed cockpit, everything needs to work together seamlessly. I love sharing the story of Sarah, a Silicon Valley CTO who revolutionized her team's efficiency by creating what she calls a "digital ecosystem." By thoughtfully connecting their project management tools, communication channels, and documentation systems, her team cut meeting time by 40% and rocketed their project completion rates up by 60%. Now that's what I call a transformation!

The Dance of Team Synchronization

Managing time across a team is like choreographing a complex dance. Everyone needs to move in harmony while maintaining their own rhythm. Take the inspiring case of Global Creative Agency, who cracked the code of remote team productivity. They discovered that the secret wasn't about controlling every minute - it was about creating the right rhythm. By establishing core collaboration hours and protecting individual focus time, they saw their productivity soar by 35%, and their team members finally found that elusive work-life balance.

Personalizing Your Productivity Style

Here's something crucial to understand: your perfect productivity system should be as unique as your fingerprint. Creative professionals thrive with different patterns than analytical workers, and that's exactly how it should be. I'm reminded of Maria, a brilliant artist who transformed her work life by breaking free from rigid schedules. Instead of fighting her natural energy flows, she embraced them, alternating between intense creative sprints and rejuvenating recovery periods.

Taming the Digital Beast

Let's talk about one of the biggest challenges we all face: digital overwhelm. The constant ping of notifications, the endless stream of emails, the multiple chat channels - it can feel like drinking from a fire hose! But there's hope. Consider Jennifer, a management consultant who turned things around by implementing what she calls "digital boundaries." By creating clear work zones and regular digital detox periods, she reclaimed her focus and actually reduced her stress levels.

Making Technology Work for You

The key to modern productivity isn't about using more tools - it's about using the right tools in the right way. A growing startup I worked with recently proved this perfectly. By thoughtfully selecting and integrating their digital tools, they cut their coordination overhead by 50% and boosted team output by 45%. The secret? They focused on tools that enhanced their natural workflow rather than complicated it.

Creating Team Harmony

Your team's productivity is like an orchestra - every section needs to play its part while contributing to the greater symphony. A creative agency I advised recently mastered this by mapping their team's energy patterns and creating designated spaces for both collaboration and deep work. The result? Better deliverables for clients and happier, more energized team members.

Remember, modern time mastery isn't about perfect schedules or rigid systems. It's about creating a flexible, intelligent approach that works for you and your team. The digital revolution has given us powerful tools - now it's time to use them wisely.

Questions to ask yourself and reflect upon:

Digital Integration & Systems

1. How well integrated are your current digital productivity tools?
2. What friction points exist in your digital workflow?
3. How effectively do you balance digital tools with analog methods?
4. What aspects of your digital system need streamlining?
5. How could better tool integration improve your productivity?

Team Coordination

1. How well do you manage time across different time zones?
2. What challenges arise in your remote collaboration?
3. How effectively do you protect focus time while staying accessible?
4. What team communication patterns need improvement?
5. How could your team's async communication be enhanced?

Work Style Adaptation

1. How well does your current system match your work style?
2. What energy patterns do you notice in your workday?
3. How effectively do you manage creative versus analytical tasks?
4. What boundaries need strengthening in your workflow?
5. How could you better align your schedule with your peak performance times?

Digital Overload

1. What triggers digital overwhelm in your work?
2. How effectively do you manage information flow?
3. What digital boundaries need reinforcement?
4. How do you maintain focus amid digital distractions?
5. What digital detox practices could benefit you?

Tool Implementation

1. How well do your current tools serve your needs?
2. What productivity stack changes would improve your workflow?
3. How effectively do you optimize existing tools?
4. What documentation systems need enhancement?
5. How could better tool selection improve team coordination?

Team Synchronization

1. How well does your team balance collaborative and independent work?
2. What team energy patterns affect productivity?
3. How effectively do you manage cross-functional coordination?
4. What team protocols need clarification or improvement?
5. How could better team synchronization reduce burnout?

CHAPTER SIXTY: UNLEASH UNSTOPPABLE PRODUCTIVITY - MASTER THE ART OF TIME BLOCKING

IN OUR MODERN world of endless notifications, constant connectivity, and competing priorities, maintaining focus and productivity often feels like an insurmountable challenge. Many of us find ourselves caught in a perpetual cycle of task-switching, responding to urgent but unimportant demands while our most important goals remain frustratingly out of reach. However, through mastering the art of time blocking, you can transform your productivity and reclaim control over your daily schedule.

The Productivity Crisis

Today's workplace demands have created an environment where interruptions are constant and deep focus seems impossible. Research shows that the average professional spends only 3 minutes on a task before being interrupted, and it takes 23 minutes to regain full concentration after each disruption. This fragmented attention comes at an enormous cost to both our productivity and wellbeing. The cumulative effect of these interruptions not only impacts our ability to complete meaningful work but also increases stress levels and reduces job satisfaction.

Understanding Time Blocking

Time blocking represents a fundamental shift in how we approach time management. Instead of reactive task-switching, this method advocates for proactive time allocation, creating dedicated periods for specific activities or projects. This structured approach aligns with how our brains naturally function, letting us harness our cognitive resources more effectively. When we dedicate specific time blocks to focused work, we create the conditions necessary for achieving ideal productivity and creativity.

The Science of Focus

Cognitive research reveals that our brains perform best when concentrating on a single type of task for an extended period. This state of deep work activates neural networks that enhance creativity, problem-solving, and learning. Time blocking creates conditions for achieving this ideal state of focused productivity. By eliminating the constant need to switch between different types of tasks, we reduce cognitive load and maximize our mental resources.

Implementation Framework

The journey to effective time blocking begins with a comprehensive assessment of your current time usage patterns. Spend a week tracking all your activities, noting how you spend each hour of your day. This audit will reveal patterns in your productivity, identify peak energy periods, and highlight common sources of distraction. Understanding these patterns is important for designing a time blocking system that works with your natural rhythms rather than against them.

Once you have a clear picture of your current time usage, the next step involves identifying your highest-priority activities and responsibilities. Consider which tasks move the needle toward your most important goals. These high-leverage activities should receive prime placement in your time blocking schedule, particularly during your peak energy periods.

Advanced Implementation

Creating an effective time blocking system requires thoughtful design and consistent execution. Begin by setting aside 60-90 minute focused blocks for your most important work, scheduling these during your identified peak energy periods. Include short breaks between blocks for renewal and buffer time for unexpected demands. This structure provides both the focus needed for deep work and the flexibility to handle inevitable disruptions.

The success of your time blocking system depends heavily on your ability to protect these designated time periods. Create both physical and digital environments that support focused work. This might mean finding a quiet workspace, turning off notifications, or using website blockers during your designated focus times. Clear communication with colleagues about your availability during blocked periods is also essential.

Sustainable Practice

As you develop your time blocking practice, consider organizing your schedule around specific themes. This might mean dedicating entire days to particular types of work or grouping similar tasks together for enhanced efficiency. This thematic approach reduces the mental energy required for context switching while maintaining enough flexibility to adapt to changing priorities.

Energy management plays an important role in successful time blocking. Pay attention to your natural energy fluctuations throughout the day and week. Schedule your most demanding tasks during peak energy periods, reserving lower energy times for routine work. Build in regular recovery periods to maintain sustainable productivity over the long term.

Overcoming Challenges

Managing interruptions effectively is crucial for maintaining the integrity of your time blocks. Develop clear protocols for handling urgent matters and create designated check-in times for communication. Having predetermined strategies for various types of disruptions helps maintain focus while remaining responsive to genuine emergencies.

Flexibility remains important even within a structured time blocking system. Build buffer time into your schedule and maintain contingency plans for when disruptions occur. Regular review and revision of your system ensure it continues to serve your evolving needs and priorities.

Measuring and Maintaining Success

Track both the quantitative and qualitative aspects of your time blocking practice. Notice improvements in task completion rates and project progress but also pay attention to the quality of your focus during blocked periods and your overall satisfaction and stress levels. These measurements provide valuable feedback for refining your approach.

Support your time blocking practice by optimizing your environment for focus and establishing clear visual cues that signal focused work time. Build accountability partnerships and share your system with key stakeholders to create a supportive ecosystem for sustained productivity.

Conclusion: Your Productivity Transformation

Time blocking represents more than just a productivity technique—it's a comprehensive approach to taking control of your time and energy. By putting this system into practice thoughtfully and consistently, you create the conditions for exceptional achievement and satisfaction in both your professional and personal life.

Begin your journey today by choosing one important priority and scheduling a protected block of time for focused work. Start small but start now. With practice and persistence, you'll discover the transformative power of working with intention rather than reaction. Your time is your most valuable asset. Through mastering time blocking, you ensure it's invested in what matters, creating the impact and results you're capable of achieving.

The path to extraordinary results starts with taking control of your minutes. Embrace the art of time blocking, and watch as your biggest goals transform from distant dreams into tangible reality. Your success depends on the choices you make today about how to invest your time and energy.

Questions to ask yourself and reflect upon:

1. What affects your productivity most?
2. How do you maintain focus?
3. What systems enhance your output?
4. How do you handle distractions?
5. What would make you more productive?

SECTION THIRTEEN: CHAPTER SUMMARY - TIME MANAGEMENT

CHAPTER 58: The Life-Changing Magic of Time Blocking

- Understanding time management crisis
- Time blocking revolution:
- Priority alignment
- Block architecture
- Protection protocols
- Buffer management
- Implementation strategies
- Advanced techniques
- Success measurement

Chapter 59: Modern Time Mastery

- Digital revolution in time management
- Building digital command center
- Team synchronization

- Personalized productivity styles
- Digital overwhelm management
- Technology integration
- Team harmony creation

Chapter 60: Unleash Unstoppable Productivity

- Productivity crisis understanding
- Time blocking science
- Implementation framework:
  - Assessment
  - Priority identification
  - System design
- Advanced implementation:
  - Environment optimization
  - Focus protection
  - Energy management
- Challenge management
- Success measurement

Key themes across chapters:

- Strategic time management
- Digital tool integration
- Focus protection
- Team coordination
- Productivity optimization
- System sustainability

∾

CONCLUSION: MASTERING YOUR POTENTIAL, ONE STEP AT A TIME

Throughout this journey, we've explored the fundamental principles and strategies for unlocking your true potential and achieving extraordinary success in all areas of life. From cultivating unshakable confidence and assertiveness to optimizing your productivity, building thriving relationships, and developing a resilient, growth-oriented mindset, you now possess a comprehensive toolkit for personal transformation.

But as we've discussed, mastery isn't a destination - it's a lifelong journey of continuous growth, learning, and pushing beyond your perceived limits. The strategies and insights you've gained are not meant to be absorbed and forgotten, but rather to be applied consistently, refined over time, and integrated deeply into your daily habits and choices.

As you move forward, remember that every challenge you face is an opportunity to strengthen your skills, expand your self-awareness, and prove your ability to overcome adversity. Every setback is a chance to cultivate resilience, adaptability, and a determination to bounce back stronger than before. And every success, no matter how small, is a testament to your incredible capacity for growth and achievement.

The path to mastering your potential is paved with consistent, purposeful action. It requires a willingness to step outside your comfort zone, to embrace discomfort as a sign of progress, and to keep pushing forward even when the way seems unclear. It demands that you continually challenge your own assumptions, seek new perspectives and experiences, and remain open to feedback and growth.

But know this: the rewards of this journey are immeasurable. As you continue to develop your potential, you'll not only achieve greater external success and impact but also a profound sense of inner fulfillment and purpose. You'll cultivate unbreakable self-confidence, forge deep and meaningful connections with others, and experience the joy of living a life aligned with your highest values and aspirations.

So, as you close this book, remember that your journey is just beginning. The real magic happens in the daily application and persistent pursuit of your goals. It happens in the quiet moments of self-reflection, the courageous steps into uncharted territory, and the unwavering commitment to your own growth and greatness.

Your potential is limitless, and your ability to shape your reality is far greater than you've ever imagined. By continuing to master the principles and strategies shared here, you'll develop the clarity, confidence, and unstoppable momentum to create a life beyond your wildest dreams.

Keep this book close as a trusted guide and ongoing resource for your journey. Refer back to it often, for information and for inspiration - to rekindle your sense of possibility, reignite your motivation, and reconnect with your deepest purpose and potential.

Success is not about perfection but rather about consistent progress and an unyielding commitment to your own growth. Embrace the challenges, celebrate the victories, and trust in your infinite capacity to learn, adapt, and overcome.

You already have everything you need to achieve greatness. Your potential is waiting to be unleashed, your dreams are ready to be realized, and your future is yours to create. Act today and keep moving forward knowing that you are capable of extraordinary things.

Master your mindset, cultivate your skills, and embrace your infinite potential. The world is waiting for your unique gifts and contributions. Step into your greatness and let your light shine brightly as an inspiration to all those around you.

Your journey to mastering your potential starts now. Embrace it with open arms and get ready to create a life beyond your most extraordinary dreams.

~

ABOUT THE AUTHOR

Rae A. Stonehouse is a Canadian born author & speaker.

His professional career as a Registered Nurse working predominantly in psychiatry / mental health spanned four decades.

Rae has embraced the principal of CANI (Constant and Never-ending Improvement) as promoted by thought leaders such as Tony Robbins and brings that philosophy to each of his publications and presentations.

Rae has dedicated the latter segment of his journey through life to overcoming his personal

inhibitions. As a 31+ year member of Toastmasters International he has systematically built his self-confidence and communicating ability.

He is passionate about sharing his lessons with his readers and listeners.

His publications thus far are of the self-help, self-improvement genre and systematically offer valuable sage advice on a specific topic.

His writing style can be described as being conversational. As an author Rae strives to have a one-to-one conversation with each of his readers, very much like having your own personal self-development coach.

Facebook: https://www.facebook.com/raestonehouse.aws

Twitter: https://twitter.com/raestonehouse

~

ALSO BY RAE A. STONEHOUSE

Visit https://liveforexcellence.store/ for a selection of personal/professional self-development books by Rae A. Stonehouse.

If you have found this book to be helpful, please leave us a warm review wherever you purchased it.

∾

THE SELF-DEVELOPMENT MINI SERIES

Introducing the books in the Self-Development Mini Series by Rae A. Stonehouse available at the Live For Excellence Store https://liveforexcellence.store

- Unlock your full problem-solving potential with **"The Problem Solver's Toolkit: Proven Techniques for Overcoming Any Challenge"** - a comprehensive guide packed with strategies, exercises, and real-world examples to help you confidently navigate any obstacle. This must-read book is part of the transformative Self-Development Mini Series.
- Unlock your innate resilience with **"The Resilience Toolkit: Practical Strategies for Thriving in Challenging Times"** - a powerful guide filled with actionable exercises and profound wisdom to help you bounce back from adversity and grow through life's toughest challenges. Chapter of the transformative "Self-Development Mini Series," this book provides a personalized roadmap for cultivating unshakable inner strength, adaptability, and a mindset for thriving no matter what obstacles you face.
- Unlock your persuasive potential with **"Mastering the Art of Persuasion: Strategies for Crafting Compelling Speeches and Presentations"** - an empowering guide that blends psychology, storytelling, and ethical communication techniques to help you craft speeches and presentations that captivate and inspire your audience. Whether you're a seasoned speaker or starting out, this book equips you with the strategies to become a master of influential communication.

- **"The Savvy Job Seeker: Proven Strategies for Landing Your Dream Job"** provides a comprehensive roadmap to navigating today's competitive job market, equipping readers with the tools and mindset they need to stand out, ace interviews, and secure the role of their dreams. Packed with practical advice, real-life examples, and empowering exercises, this book is an essential guide for anyone seeking to unlock their full potential and achieve long-term career success.
- Unlock exponential growth through the power of authentic relationships with **"Networking Unleashed: Creating Exponential Growth Through Connections"** - this transformative guide redefines networking as a mindset for cultivating meaningful connections that enrich your personal and professional life. Discover how to become a "super-connector," leverage your unique strengths, and harness the extraordinary ripple effect of your network.
- Unlock your potential as a confident, impactful leader with **"Leading with Confidence: A Guide to Developing Assertiveness for Impactful Leadership"** - a powerful roadmap to mastering assertive communication, providing constructive feedback, setting boundaries, delegating effectively, and cultivating an inclusive team culture. This transformative guide equips you with practical strategies and relatable insights to inspire those around you and drive meaningful change.
- Transform conflicts into opportunities for growth with **"Resolving Conflicts with Confidence: Strategies for Effective Communication and Assertiveness"** - your comprehensive guide to mastering assertive communication, active listening, and collaborative problem-solving skills. This powerful resource empowers you to navigate difficult conversations with poise and achieve mutually beneficial resolutions.
- **"Mastering Your Emotions: Unlocking the Power of Emotional Intelligence"** guides you on a transformative journey to understand, manage, and harness your emotions for personal growth and success. Through practical strategies and insightful exercises, this book empowers you to develop emotional intelligence, build stronger relationships, and achieve greater fulfillment in all areas of life.
- Unleash your highest potential with **"Rising Above: Transforming Life's Challenges into Opportunities for Growth"** - a powerful guide to cultivating a growth mindset, building resilience, and transforming life's obstacles into profound opportunities for self-discovery and

positive change. This empowering book provides a comprehensive roadmap for turning adversities into catalysts for lifelong learning, adaptability, and personal mastery.

- Unlock your productivity potential with **"Mastering Your Minutes: A Guide to Effective Time Management"** by Rae A. Stonehouse - a transformative roadmap that empowers you to take control of your time, meet your goals, and create a life of balance and fulfillment. This powerful book, part of the acclaimed Self-Development Mini Series, offers practical strategies, insightful exercises, and a holistic approach to help you master effective time management and thrive in all aspects of your life.

- Unlock your true potential with **"Conquering Procrastination: A Step-by-Step Guide to Unleashing Your Productivity"** - a powerful resource that equips you with practical strategies to overcome procrastination, embrace a growth mindset, and develop the focus and resilience needed to meet your goals. This transformative guide gives you invaluable tools to build accountability, cultivate self-compassion, and ultimately conquer the barriers that hold you back from reaching new heights.

- Embrace the transformative power of change with **"Embracing Change: Unlocking Your Potential in Life's Ever-Shifting Landscape"** - a profound guide to navigating life's pivots with resilience, cultivating a growth mindset, and unlocking your full potential. Chapter of the inspiring Self-Development Mini Book series, this empowering read provides a roadmap for personal growth and fulfillment amidst life's ever evolving landscape.

- Unleash your infinite potential with **"Unshackled: Breaking Free from the Chains of Limiting Beliefs"** - a powerful guide to identifying and overcoming the self-limiting beliefs holding you back from living your biggest, boldest life. Through profound insights, practical exercises, and inspiring real-life stories, you'll cultivate unshakable self-belief and gain the courage to create a reality greater than your wildest dreams.

- Unlock your full potential with **"Goal Setting Simplified: A No-Nonsense Guide to Achieving"** - a powerful roadmap for clarifying your vision, taking purposeful action, and simplifying your journey to success through straightforward strategies and Rae A. Stonehouse's profound wisdom. This game-changing guide will equip you with the tools to set achievable goals, develop laser-focus, stay motivated through obstacles, and embrace an adaptable mindset to turn your biggest dreams into reality.

- Unlock your full potential with **"Goal Achievement Essentials: Tools, Tips & Techniques,"** a powerful guide packed with essential strategies for setting clear goals, maximizing productivity, overcoming procrastination, and consistently achieving your dreams. This motivating book provides a comprehensive blueprint for goal mastery through hands-on exercises, real-life examples, and Rae A. Stonehouse's decades of wisdom cultivating human potential.

- Master the transformative power of positive thinking with **"Mind Over Matter: Transforming Your Life Through the Power of Positive Thinking"** - an empowering guide packed with practical strategies, scientific insights, and motivational stories to help you reshape your mindset, reduce stress, and cultivate a more fulfilling life. This book is your key to unlocking joy, resilience, and personal growth through the incredible potential of your thoughts.